Unity 4.x Game AI Programming

Learn and implement game AI in Unity3D with a lot of sample projects and next-generation techniques to use in your Unity3D projects

Aung Sithu Kyaw

Clifford Peters

Thet Naing Swe

PUBLISHING

BIRMINGHAM - MUMBAI

Unity 4.x Game AI Programming

First published: July 2013

Production Reference: 1160713

Published by Packt Publishing Ltd.
Livery Place
35 Livery Street
Birmingham B3 2PB, UK.

ISBN 978-1-84969-340-0

www.packtpub.com

Cover Image by Artie Ng (artherng@yahoo.com.au)

Credits

Authors
Aung Sithu Kyaw
Clifford Peters
Thet Naing Swe

Reviewers
Julien Lange
Clifford Peters

Acquisition Editor
Kartikey Pandey

Lead Technical Editor
Arun Nadar

Technical Editors
Shashank Desai
Krishnaveni Haridas
Rikita Poojari

Project Coordinator
Anurag Banerjee

Proofreaders
Maria Gould
Paul Hindle
Aaron Nash

Indexer
Monica Ajmera Mehta

Graphics
Ronak Dhruv
Abhinash Sahu

Production Coordinator
Nilesh R. Mohite

Cover Work
Nilesh R. Mohite

About the Authors

Aung Sithu Kyaw is originally from Myanmar, (Burma) and has over seven years of experience in the software industry. His main interests include game-play programming, startups, entrepreneurship, writing, and sharing knowledge. He holds a Master of Science degree from Nanyang Technological University (NTU), Singapore, majoring in Digital Media Technology. Over the past few years, he has worked as a Research Programmer at INSEAD, Sr. Game Programmer at Playware Studios Asia, Singapore, and lastly as a Research Associate at NTU. In 2011, Aung co-founded Rival Edge Pte Ltd., a Singapore-based interactive digital media company that provides a technical consultancy service to creative agencies and also produces social mobile games. Visit `http://rivaledge.sg` for more information. Aung is the co-author of *Irrlicht 1.7 Realtime 3D Engine Beginner's Guide*, *Packt Publishing*, and is also a visiting lecturer at NTU conducting workshops on game design and development using Unity3D.He can be followed on Twitter `@aungsithu` and by using his LinkedIn profile `linkedin.com/in/aungsithu`.

Thanks to my co-authors who worked with me really hard on this book despite their busy schedules and got this book published. Also, thanks to the team at Packt Publishing for helping us in the production of this book. And finally, thanks to the awesome guys at Unity3D for building this amazing toolset and for making it affordable to indie game developers.

Clifford Peters is a programmer and a computer scientist. He has reviewed the following *Packt Publishing* books: *Unity Game Development Essentials, Unity 3D Game Development by Example Beginner's Guide, Unity 3 Game Development Hotshot, Unity 3.x Game Development by Example Beginner's Guide, Unity iOS Game Development Beginner's Guide*, and *Unity iOS Essentials*.

Thet Naing Swe is the co-founder and Chief Creative Director of Rival Edge Pte Ltd., based in Singapore. He graduated from the University of Central Lancashire where he majored in Game Design and Development and started his career as a game programmer at the UK-based Code Monkeys studios. He relocated to Singapore in 2010 and worked as a graphics programmer at Nanyang Technological University (NTU) on a cinematic research project together with Aung. Currently at Rival Edge, he's responsible for interactive digital media consulting projects mainly using Unity3D as well as making social mobile games for a casual audience. He can be reached via `thetnswe@rivaledge.sg`.

I would like to thank the whole team at Packt Publishing for keeping track of all the logistics and making sure the book was published. I really appreciate that. Besides that, I'd like to thank my parents for raising and supporting me all these years and letting me pursue my dream to become a game developer. Without all of your support, I wouldn't be here today.

And finally, huge thanks to my wife, May Thandar Aung, for allowing me to work on this book after office hours, late at night, and weekends. Without your understanding and support, this book would have been delayed for another year. I'm grateful to have your support with me whatever I do. Love you.

About the Reviewer

Julien Lange is a 32 year old IT expert in Software Engineering. He started to develop on Amstrad CPC464 with the BASIC language when he was 7. He learned Visual Basic soon after, then VB.NET and C#. For several years until the end of his studies, he developed and maintained several PHP and ASP.NET e-business websites. After his graduation, he continued to learn more and more about software like Architecture, Project management always acquiring new skills.

It was at work while talking with a colleague in August 2009 and after discovering the high potential of iPhone games and softwares that he decided to find an improved game engine allowing him to concentrate only on the main purpose of developing a game and not a game engine. After trying two other game engines, his choice was Unity 3D thanks to its compatibility with C# and its high frame rate performance on iPhone. In addition to his main work, he opened iXGaming.com as self-employed in December 2010 and launched several applications on the AppStore, such as Cartoon TV, GalaXia, and so on.

I would like to thank my wife for allowing me to take some time to review books on my computer. I would also like to thank Frederic for all the work we completed together with Unity. I would also like to thank all the current Unity Asset Store customers who are using my published assets and scripts. New services are coming very soon on the Asset Store.

Finally, I would like to thank my family, my friends, and colleagues including Stephane D., Chakib L., Christelle P., Raphael D., Alain D.L, Sebastien P., and Emmanuel.

www.PacktPub.com

Support files, eBooks, discount offers and more

You might want to visit www.PacktPub.com for support files and downloads related to your book.

Did you know that Packt offers eBook versions of every book published, with PDF and ePub files available? You can upgrade to the eBook version at www.PacktPub.com and as a print book customer, you are entitled to a discount on the eBook copy. Get in touch with us at service@packtpub.com for more details.

At www.PacktPub.com, you can also read a collection of free technical articles, sign up for a range of free newsletters and receive exclusive discounts and offers on Packt books and eBooks.

http://PacktLib.PacktPub.com

Do you need instant solutions to your IT questions? PacktLib is Packt's online digital book library. Here, you can access, read and search across Packt's entire library of books.

Why Subscribe?

- Fully searchable across every book published by Packt
- Copy and paste, print and bookmark content
- On demand and accessible via web browser

Free Access for Packt account holders

If you have an account with Packt atwww.PacktPub.com, you can use this to access PacktLib today and view nine entirely free books. Simply use your login credentials for immediate access.

To the loving memory of my father, U Aung Than, and to my little girl, who brings a new perspective to my life

–dedicated by Aung Sithu Kyaw

Table of Contents

Preface   **1**

Chapter 1: Introduction to AI   **5**

   Artificial Intelligence (AI)   **5**
   AI in games   **6**
   AI techniques   **7**
      Finite State Machines (FSM)   7
      Random and probability in AI   9
      The sensor system   10
         Polling   10
         The messaging system   10
      Flocking, swarming, and herding   11
      Path following and steering   12
      A* pathfinding   13
      A navigation mesh   20
      The behavior trees   23
      Locomotion   25
      Dijkstra's algorithm   28
   Summary   **28**

Chapter 2: Finite State Machines   **29**

   The player's tank   **30**
      The PlayerTankController class   30
      Initialization   31
         Shooting bullet   32
         Controlling the tank   32
   The bullet class   **35**
   Setting up waypoints   **37**
   The abstract FSM class   **38**

The enemy tank AI — **39**
  The patrol state — 42
  The chase state — 43
  The attack state — 44
  The dead state — 45
    Taking damage — 46
Using an FSM framework — **47**
  The AdvanceFSM class — 48
  The FSMState class — 49
  The state classes — 50
    The PatrolState class — 50
  The NPCTankController class — 52
Summary — **54**

Chapter 3: Random and Probability — **55**
  Random — **56**
    Random class — 56
      Simple random dice game — 57
  Definition of probability — **58**
    Independent and related events — 59
    Conditional probability — 59
      A loaded dice — 60
  Character personalities — **61**
  FSM with probability — **62**
  Dynamic AI — **64**
  Demo slot machine — **65**
    Random slot machine — 65
    Weighted probability — 69
      Near miss — 73
  Summary — **74**

Chapter 4: Implementing Sensors — **75**
  Basic sensory systems — **76**
  Scene setup — **76**
  Player tank and aspect — **78**
    Player tank — 79
    Aspect — 81
  AI character — **81**
    Sense — 83
    Perspective — 83
    Touch — 86
  Testing — **88**
  Summary — **88**

Chapter 5: Flocking   89
Flocking from Unity's Island Demo   89
Individual Behavior   90
Controller   97
Alternative implementation   99
FlockController   101
Summary   106

Chapter 6: Path Following and Steering Behaviors   107
Following a path   108
Path script   110
Path follower   111
Avoiding obstacles   114
Adding a custom layer   116
Obstacle avoidance   117
Summary   121

Chapter 7: A* Pathfinding   123
A* algorithm revisit   123
Implementation   124
Node   125
PriorityQueue   126
GridManager   127
AStar   132
TestCode class   135
Scene setup   137
Testing   141
Summary   142

Chapter 8: Navigation Mesh   143
Introduction   144
Setting up the map   144
Navigation Static   145
Baking the navigation mesh   145
Nav Mesh Agent   146
Updating agents' destinations   148
Scene with slope   149
NavMeshLayers   151
Off Mesh Links   153
Generated Off Mesh Links   154
Manual Off Mesh Links   156
Summary   158

Chapter 9: Behavior Trees	**159**
Behave plugin	**160**
Workflow	**161**
Action	**164**
Interfacing with the script	**166**
Decorator	**169**
Behave debugger	**171**
Sequence	**172**
Exploring Behave results	**173**
Selector	**175**
Priority selector	**177**
Parallel	**179**
Reference	**181**
The Robots versus Aliens project	**181**
Summary	**184**
Chapter 10: Putting It All Together	**185**
Scene setup	**186**
Tags and layers	188
Vehicles	**189**
Player car controller	190
AI Car Controller	192
Finite State Machines (FSMs)	194
Patrol state	195
Chase state	197
Attack state	198
Weapons	**199**
Gun	200
Bullet	201
Launcher	203
Missile	205
Summary	**208**
Index	**209**

Preface

This book is meant to help you to incorporate various Artificial Intelligence techniques into your games. We will discuss decision techniques such as Finite State Machines and Behavior Trees. We will also look at movement, obstacle avoidance, and flocking. We also show how to follow a path, how to create a path using the A* pathfinding algorithm, and then how to reach a destination using a navigation mesh. As a bonus we will go into detail about random and probability, and then incorporate these ideas into a final project.

What this book covers

Chapter 1, *Introduction to AI*, talks about what Artificial Intelligence is, and how it is used in games. Also, we talk about various techniques used to implement AI into games.

Chapter 2, *Finite State Machines*, discusses a way of simplifying how we manage the decisions, which AI needs to make. We use FSMs to determine how AI behaves in a particular state and how it transitions to other states.

Chapter 3, *Random and Probability*, discusses the basics behind probability, and how to change the probability of a particular outcome. Then we look at how to add randomness to our game to make the AI less predictable.

Chapter 4, *Implementing Sensors*, looks at where we should make our character aware of the world around them. With the ability of our characters to see and hear, they will know when an enemy is nearby and will know when to attack.

Chapter 5, *Flocking*, discusses a situation where many objects travel together as a group. We will look at two different ways to implement flocking, and how it can be used to make objects move together.

Chapter 6, *Path Following and Steering Behaviors*, looks at how AI characters can follow a path provided to reach a destination. Then we look at how AI characters can find a target without knowing a path, and by moving towards a goal while avoiding.

Chapter 7, A* Pathfinding, discusses a popular algorithm, which is used to find the best route from a given location to a target location. With A*, we scan the terrain and find the best path that leads us to the goal.

Chapter 8, Navigation Mesh, discusses using the power of Unity to make pathfinding easier to implement. By creating a Navigation Mesh (this requires Unity Pro), we will be able to represent the scene around us better then we could using tiles and the A* algorithm.

Chapter 9, Behavior Trees, expands upon Finite State Machines into something we can use for even the most complex of games. We will be using the free plugin Behave to help us create and manage Behavior Trees in Unity.

Chapter 10, Putting It All Together, takes various elements of what we have learned throughout the book and putting together one last project. From here you will be able to apply the remaining AI elements we learned and create an impressive vehicle battle game.

What you need for this book

The main requirement for this book is having Unity Version 3.5 or higher installed. *Chapter 8, Navigation Mesh* talks about creating a Navigation Mesh, something that requires Unity Pro. In *Chapter 9, Behavior Trees* we download Behave, a free Behavior Tree plugin, which requires an account with the Unity Store. Both of these requirements are optional because the assets that come with this book already have the Navigation Mesh generated and the Behave plugin.

Who this book is for

This book is for anyone who wants to learn about incorporating AI into games. This book is intended for users with prior experience of using Unity. We will be coding in C#, so some familiarity with this language is expected.

Conventions

In this book, you will find a number of styles of text that distinguish between different kinds of information. Here are some examples of these styles, and an explanation of their meaning.

Code words in text are shown as follows: "The `AdvanceFSM` class basically manages all the `FSMState`(s) implemented, and keeps updated with the transitions and the current state."

A block of code is set as follows:

```
using UnityEngine;
using System.Collections;
using System.Collections.Generic;

public enum Transition
{
    None = 0,
    SawPlayer,
    ReachPlayer,
    LostPlayer,
    NoHealth,
}
```

New terms and **important words** are shown in bold. Words that you see on the screen, in menus or dialog boxes for example, appear in the text like this: "Our **Tank** object is basically a simple **Mesh** with a **Rigidbody** component."

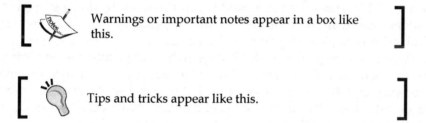

> Warnings or important notes appear in a box like this.

> Tips and tricks appear like this.

Reader feedback

Feedback from our readers is always welcome. Let us know what you think about this book—what you liked or may have disliked. Reader feedback is important for us to develop titles that you really get the most out of.

To send us general feedback, simply send an e-mail to feedback@packtpub.com, and mention the book title via the subject of your message.

If there is a topic that you have expertise in and you are interested in either writing or contributing to a book, see our author guide on www.packtpub.com/authors.

Customer support

Now that you are the proud owner of a Packt book, we have a number of things to help you to get the most from your purchase.

Downloading the example code

You can download the example code files for all Packt books you have purchased from your account at http://www.packtpub.com. If you purchased this book elsewhere, you can visit http://www.packtpub.com/support and register to have the files e-mailed directly to you.

Downloading the color images of this book

We also provide you a PDF file that has color images of the screenshots/diagrams used in this book. The color images will help you better understand the changes in the output. You can download this file from: http://www.packtpub.com/sites/default/files/downloads/3400OT_ColoredImages.pdf

Errata

Although we have taken every care to ensure the accuracy of our content, mistakes do happen. If you find a mistake in one of our books—maybe a mistake in the text or the code—we would be grateful if you would report this to us. By doing so, you can save other readers from frustration and help us improve subsequent versions of this book. If you find any errata, please report them by visiting http://www.packtpub.com/submit-errata, selecting your book, clicking on the **errata submission form** link, and entering the details of your errata. Once your errata are verified, your submission will be accepted and the errata will be uploaded on our website, or added to any list of existing errata, under the Errata section of that title. Any existing errata can be viewed by selecting your title from http://www.packtpub.com/support.

Piracy

Piracy of copyright material on the Internet is an ongoing problem across all media. At Packt, we take the protection of our copyright and licenses very seriously. If you come across any illegal copies of our works, in any form, on the Internet, please provide us with the location address or website name immediately so that we can pursue a remedy.

Please contact us at copyright@packtpub.com with a link to the suspected pirated material.

We appreciate your help in protecting our authors, and our ability to bring you valuable content.

Questions

You can contact us at questions@packtpub.com if you are having a problem with any aspect of the book, and we will do our best to address it.

1
Introduction to AI

This chapter will give you a little background on artificial intelligence in academic, traditional domains, and game specific applications. We'll learn how the application and implementation of AI in games is different from other domains, and the important and special requirements for AI in games. We'll also explore the basic techniques of AI used in games. This chapter will serve as a reference for later chapters, where we'll implement those AI techniques in Unity.

Artificial Intelligence (AI)

Living organisms such as animals and humans have some sort of intelligence that helps us in making a particular decision to perform something. On the other hand, computers are just electronic devices that can accept data, perform logical and mathematical operations at high speeds, and output the results. So, **Artificial Intelligence (AI)** is essentially the subject of making computers able to think and decide like living organisms to perform specific operations.

So, apparently this is a huge subject. And there's no way that such a small book will be able to cover everything related to AI. But it is really important to understand the basics of AI being used in different domains. AI is just a general term; its implementations and applications are different for different purposes, solving different sets of problems.

Before we move on to game-specific techniques, we'll take a look at the following research areas in AI applications:

- **Computer vision**: It is the ability to take visual input from sources such as videos and cameras, and analyze them to do particular operations such as facial recognition, object recognition, and optical-character recognition.

- **Natural language processing (NLP)**: It is the ability that allows a machine to read and understand the languages, as we normally write and speak. The problem is that the languages we use today are difficult for machines to understand. There are many different ways to say the same thing, and the same sentence can have different meanings according to the context. NLP is an important step for machines, since they need to understand the languages and expressions we use, before they can process them and respond accordingly. Fortunately, there's an enormous amount of data sets available on the Web that can help researchers to do automatic analysis of a language.

- **Common sense reasoning**: This is a technique that our brains can easily use to draw answers even from the domains we don't fully understand. Common sense knowledge is a usual and common way for us to attempt certain questions, since our brains can mix and interplay between the context, background knowledge, and language proficiency. But making machines to apply such knowledge is very complex, and still a major challenge for researchers.

AI in games

Game AI needs to complement the quality of a game. For that we need to understand the fundamental requirement that every game must have. The answer should be easy. It is the fun factor. So, what makes a game fun to play? This is the subject of game design, and a good reference is *The Art of Game Design* by *Jesse Schell*. Let's attempt to tackle this question without going deep into game design topics. We'll find that a challenging game is indeed fun to play. Let me repeat: it's about making a game challenging. This means the game should not be so difficult that it's impossible for the player to beat the opponent, or too easy to win. Finding the right challenge level is the key to make a game fun to play.

And that's where the AI kicks in. The role of AI in games is to make it fun by providing challenging opponents to compete, and interesting **non-player characters (NPCs)** that behave realistically inside the game world. So, the objective here is not to replicate the whole thought process of humans or animals, but to make the NPCs seem intelligent by reacting to the changing situations inside the game world in a way that makes sense to the player.

The reason that we don't want to make the AI system in games so computationally expensive is that the processing power required for AI calculations needs to be shared between other operations such as graphic rendering and physics simulation. Also, don't forget that they are all happening in real time, and it's also really important to achieve a steady framerate throughout the game. There were even attempts to create dedicated processor for AI calculations (AI Seek's Intia Processor). With the ever-increasing processing power, we now have more and more room for AI calculations. However, like all the other disciplines in game development, optimizing AI calculations remains a huge challenge for the AI developers.

AI techniques

In this section, we'll walk through some of the AI techniques being used in different types of games. We'll learn how to implement each of these features in Unity in the upcoming chapters. Since this book is not focused on AI techniques itself, but the implementation of those techniques inside Unity, we won't go into too much detail about these techniques here. So, let's just take it as a crash course, before actually going into implementation. If you want to learn more about AI for games, there are some really great books out there, such as *Programming Game AI by Example* by *Mat Buckland* and *Artificial Intelligence for Games* by *Ian Millington* and *John Funge*. The *AI Game Programming Wisdom* series also contain a lot of useful resources and articles on the latest AI techniques.

Finite State Machines (FSM)

Finite State Machines (FSM) can be considered as one of the simplest AI model form, and are commonly used in the majority of games. A state machine basically consists of a finite number of states that are connected in a graph by the transitions between them. A game entity starts with an initial state, and then looks out for the events and rules that will trigger a transition to another state. A game entity can only be in exactly one state at any given time.

For example, let's take a look at an AI guard character in a typical shooting game. Its states could be as simple as patrolling, chasing, and shooting.

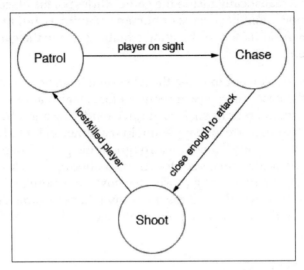

Simple FSM of an AI guard character

There are basically four components in a simple FSM:

- **States**: This component defines a set of states that a game entity or an NPC can choose from (patrol, chase, and shoot)
- **Transitions**: This component defines relations between different states
- **Rules**: This component is used to trigger a state transition (player on sight, close enough to attack, and lost/killed player)
- **Events**: This is the component, which will trigger to check the rules (guard's visible area, distance with the player, and so on)

So, a monster in Quake 2 might have the following states: standing, walking, running, dodging, attacking, idle, and searching.

FSMs are widely used in game AI especially, because they are really easy to implement and more than enough for both simple and somewhat complex games. Using simple `if/else` statements or switch statements, we can easily implement an FSM. It can get messy, as we start to have more states and more transitions. We'll look at how to manage a simple FSM in the next chapter.

Random and probability in AI

Imagine an enemy bot in an FPS game that can always kill the player with a headshot, an opponent in a racing game that always chooses the best route, and overtakes without collision with any obstacle. Such a level of intelligence will make the game so difficult that it becomes almost impossible to win. On the other hand, imagine an AI enemy that always chooses the same route to follow, or tries to escape from the player. AI controlled entities behaving the same way every time the player encounters them, makes the game predictable and easy to win.

Both of the previous situations obviously affect the fun aspect of the game, and make the player feel like the game is not challenging or fair enough anymore. One way to fix this sort of perfect AI and stupid AI is to introduce some errors in their intelligence. In games, randomness and probabilities are applied in the decision making process of AI calculations. The following are the main situations when we would want to let our AI entities change a random decision:

- **Non-intentional**: This situation is sometimes a game agent, or perhaps an NPC might need to make a decision randomly, just because it doesn't have enough information to make a perfect decision, and/or it doesn't really matter what decision it makes. Simply making a decision randomly and hoping for the best result is the way to go in such a situation.

- **Intentional**: This situation is for perfect AI and stupid AI. As we discussed in the previous examples, we will need to add some randomness purposely, just to make them more realistic, and also to match the difficulty level that the player is comfortable with. Such randomness and probability could be used for things such as hit probabilities, plus or minus random damage on top of base damage. Using randomness and probability we can add a sense of realistic uncertainty to our game and make our AI system somewhat unpredictable.

We can also use probability to define different classes of AI characters. Let's look at the hero characters from **Defense of the Ancient (DotA)**, which is a popular action **real-time strategy (RTS)** game mode of Warcraft III. There are three categories of heroes based on the three main attributes: strength, intelligence, and agility. Strength is the measure of the physical power of the hero, while intellect relates to how well the hero can control spells and magic. Agility defines a hero's ability to avoid attacks and attack quickly. An AI hero from the strength category will have the ability to do more damage during close combat, while an intelligence hero will have more chance of success to score higher damage using spells and magic. Carefully balancing the randomness and probability between different classes and heroes, makes the game a lot more challenging, and makes DotA a lot fun to play.

The sensor system

Our AI characters need to know about their surroundings, and the world they are interacting with, in order to make a particular decision. Such information could be as follows:

- **Position of the player**: This information is used to decide whether to attack or chase, or keep patrolling
- **Buildings and objects nearby**: This information is used to hide or take cover
- **Player's health and its own health**: This remaining information is used to decide whether to retreat or advance
- **Location of resources on the map in an RTS game**: This information is used to occupy and collect resources, required for constructing and producing other units

As you can see, it could vary a lot depending on the type of game we are trying to build. So, how do we collect that information?

Polling

One method to collect such information is polling. We can simply do `if/else` or `switch` checks in the `FixedUpdate` method of our AI character. AI character just polls the information they are interested in from the game world, does the checks, and takes action accordingly. Polling methods works great, if there aren't too many things to check. However, some characters might not need to poll the world states every frame. Different characters might require different polling rates. So, usually in larger games with more complex AI systems, we need to deploy an event-driven method using a global messaging system.

The messaging system

AI does decision making in response to the events in the world. The events are communicated between the AI entity and the player, the world, or the other AI entities through a messaging system. For example, when the player attacks an enemy unit from a group of patrol guards, the other AI units need to know about this incident as well, so that they can start searching for and attacking the player. If we were using the polling method, our AI entities will need to check the state of all the other AI entities, in order to know about this incident. But with an event-driven messaging system, we can implement this in a more manageable and scalable way. The AI characters interested in a particular event can be registered as listeners, and if that event happens, our messaging system will broadcast to all listeners. The AI entities can then proceed to take appropriate actions, or perform further checks.

The event-driven system does not necessarily provide faster mechanism than polling. But it provides a convenient, central checking system that senses the world and informs the interested AI agents, rather than each individual agent having to check the same event in every frame. In reality, both polling and messaging system are used together most of the time. For example, AI might poll for more detailed information when it receives an event from the messaging system.

Flocking, swarming, and herding

Many living beings such as birds, fish, insects, and land animals perform certain operations such as moving, hunting, and foraging in groups. They stay and hunt in groups, because it makes them stronger and safer from predators than pursuing goals individually. So, let's say you want a group of birds flocking, swarming around in the sky; it'll cost too much time and effort for animators to design the movement and animations of each bird. But if we apply some simple rules for each bird to follow, we can achieve emergent intelligence of the whole group with complex, global behavior.

One pioneer of this concept is *Craig Reynolds*, who presented such a flocking algorithm in his *SIGGRAPH* paper, 1987, *Flocks, Herds and Schools – A Distributed Behavioral Model*. He coined the term "boid" that sounds like "bird", but referring to a "bird-like" object. He proposed three simple rules to apply to each unit, which are as follows:

- **Separation**: This rule is used to maintain a minimum distance with neighboring boids to avoid hitting them
- **Alignment**: This rule is used to align itself with the average direction of its neighbors, and then move in the same velocity with them as a flock
- **Cohesion**: This step is used to maintain a minimum distance with the group's center of mass

These three simple rules are all that we need to implement a realistic and a fairly complex flocking behavior for birds. They can also be applied to group behaviors of any other entity type with little or no modifications. We'll examine how to implement such a flocking system in Unity in *Chapter 5, Flocking*.

Downloading the color images of this book

We also provide you a PDF file that has color images of the screenshots/diagrams used in this book. The color images will help you better understand the changes in the output. You can download this file from: http://www.packtpub.com/sites/default/files/downloads/3400OT_ColoredImages.pdf

Path following and steering

Sometimes we want our AI characters to roam around in the game world, following a roughly guided or thoroughly defined path. For example in a racing game, the AI opponents need to navigate on the road. And the decision-making algorithms such as our flocking boid algorithm discussed already, can only do well in making decisions. But in the end, it all comes down to dealing with actual movements and steering behaviors. Steering behaviors for AI characters have been in research topics for a couple of decades now. One notable paper in this field is *Steering Behaviors for Autonomous Characters*, again by *Craig Reynolds*, presented in 1999 at the **Game Developers Conference (GDC)**. He categorized steering behaviors into the following three layers:

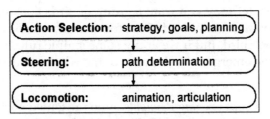

Hierarchy of motion behaviors

Let me quote the original example from his paper to understand these three layers:

"Consider, for example, some cowboys tending a herd of cattle out on the range. A cow wanders away from the herd. The trail boss tells a cowboy to fetch the stray. The cowboy says "giddy-up" to his horse, and guides it to the cow, possibly avoiding obstacles along the way. In this example, the trail boss represents action selection, noticing that the state of the world has changed (a cow left the herd), and setting a goal (retrieve the stray). The steering level is represented by the cowboy who decomposes the goal into a series of simple sub goals (approach the cow, avoid obstacles, and retrieve the cow). A sub goal corresponds to a steering behavior for the cowboy-and-horse team. Using various control signals (vocal commands, spurs, and reins), the cowboy steers his horse towards the target. In general terms, these signals express concepts like go faster, go slower, turn right, turn left, and so on. The horse implements the locomotion level. Taking the cowboy's control signals as input, the horse moves in the indicated direction. This motion is the result of a complex interaction of the horse's visual perception, its sense of balance, and its muscles applying torques to the joints of its skeleton."

Then he presented how to design and implement some common and simple steering behaviors for individual AI characters and pairs. Such behaviors include seek and flee, pursue and evade, wander, arrival, obstacle avoidance, wall following, and path following. We'll implement some of those behaviors in Unity in *Chapter 6, Path Following and Steering Behaviors*.

A* pathfinding

There are many games where you can find monsters or enemies that follow the player, or go to a particular point while avoiding obstacles. For example, let's take a look at a typical RTS game. You can select a group of units and click a location where you want them to move or click on the enemy units to attack them. Your units then need to find a way to reach the goal without colliding with the obstacles. The enemy units also need to be able to do the same. Obstacles could be different for different units. For example, an air force unit might be able to pass over a mountain, while the ground or artillery units need to find a way around it.

A* (pronounced "A star") is a pathfinding algorithm widely used in games, because of its performance and accuracy. Let's take a look at an example to see how it works. Let's say we want our unit to move from point A to point B, but there's a wall in the way, and it can't go straight towards the target. So, it needs to find a way to point B while avoiding the wall.

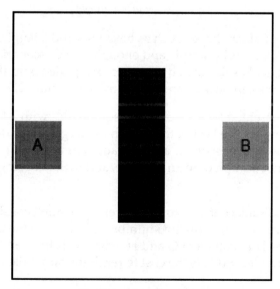

Top-down view of our map

We are looking at a simple 2D example. But the same idea can be applied to 3D environments. In order to find the path from point A to point B, we need to know more about the map such as the position of obstacles. For that we can split our whole map into small tiles, representing the whole map in a grid format, as shown in the following figure:

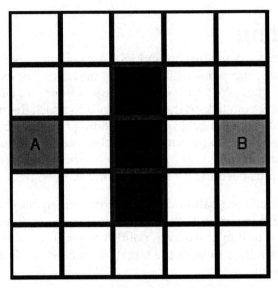

Map represented in a 2D grid

The tiles can also be of other shapes such as hexagons and triangles. But we'll just use square tiles here, as that's quite simple and enough for our scenario. Representing the whole map in a grid, makes the search area more simplified, and this is an important step in pathfinding. We can now reference our map in a small 2D array.

Our map is now represented by a 5 x 5 grid of square tiles with a total of 25 tiles. We can start searching for the best path to reach the target. How do we do this? By calculating the movement score of each tile adjacent to the starting tile, which is a tile on the map not occupied by an obstacle, and then choosing the tile with the lowest cost.

There are four possible adjacent tiles to the player, if we don't consider the diagonal movements. Now, we need to know two numbers to calculate the movement score for each of those tiles. Let's call them G and H, where G is the cost of movement from starting tile to current tile, and H is the cost to reach the target tile from current tile.

By adding G and H, we can get the final score of that tile; let's call it F. So we'll be using this formula: F = G + H.

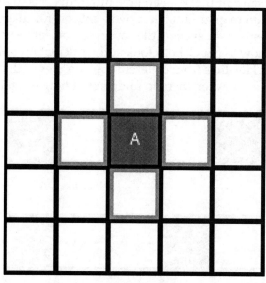

Valid adjacent tiles

In this example, we'll be using a simple method called **Manhattan length** (also known as Taxicab geometry), in which we just count the total number of tiles between the starting tile and the target tile to know the distance between them.

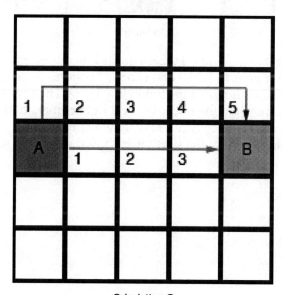

Calculating G

The preceding figure shows the calculations of G with two different paths. We just add one (which is the cost to move one tile) to the previous tile's G score to get the current G score of the current tile. We can give different costs to different tiles. For example, we might want to give a higher movement cost for diagonal movements (if we are considering them), or to specific tiles occupied by, let's say a pond or a muddy road. Now we know how to get G. Let's look at the calculation of H. The following figure shows different H values from different starting tiles to the target tile. You can try counting the squares between them to understand how we get those values.

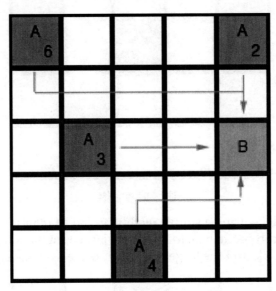

Calculating H

So, now we know how to get G and H. Let's go back to our original example to figure out the shortest path from A to B. We first choose the starting tile, and then determine the valid adjacent tiles, as shown in the following figure. Then we calculate the G and H scores of each tile, shown in the lower-left and right corners of the tile respectively. And then the final score F, which is G + H is shown at the top-left corner. Obviously, the tile to the immediate right of the start tile has got the lowest F score.

So, we choose this tile as our next movement, and store the previous tile as its parent. This parent stuff will be useful later, when we trace back our final path.

Starting position

From the current tile, we do the similar process again, determining valid adjacent tiles. This time there are only two valid adjacent tiles at the top and bottom. The left tile is a starting tile, which we've already examined, and the obstacle occupies the right tile. We calculate the G, the H, and then the F score of those new adjacent tiles. This time we have four tiles on our map with all having the same score, six. So, which one do we choose? We can choose any of them. It doesn't really matter in this example, because we'll eventually find the shortest path with whichever tile we choose, if they have the same score. Usually, we just choose the tile added most recently to our adjacent list. This is because later we'll be using some sort of data structure, such as a list to store those tiles that are being considered for the next move. So, accessing the tile most recently added to that list could be faster than searching through the list to reach a particular tile that was added previously.

In this demo, we'll just randomly choose the tile for our next test, just to prove that it can actually find the shortest path.

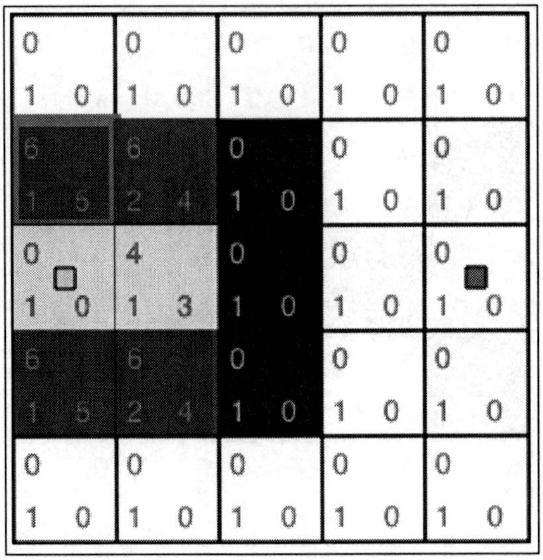

Second step

So, we choose this tile, which is highlighted with a red border. Again we examine the adjacent tiles. In this step, there's only one new adjacent tile with a calculated F score of 8. So, the lowest score right now is still 6. We can choose any tile with the score 6.

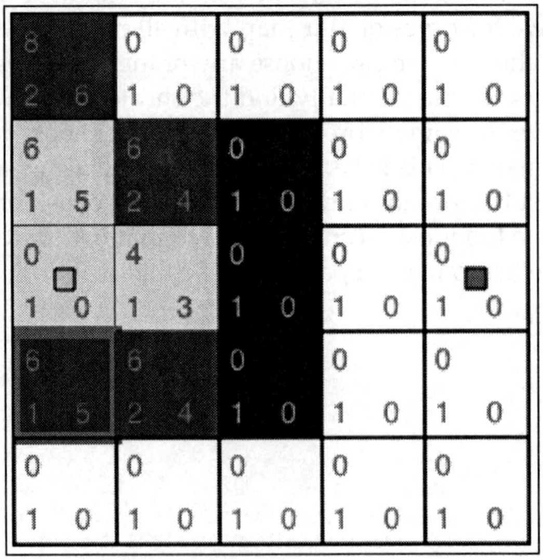

Third step

So, we choose a tile randomly from all the tiles with the score 6. If we repeat this process until we reach our target tile, we'll end up with a board complete with all the scores for each valid tile.

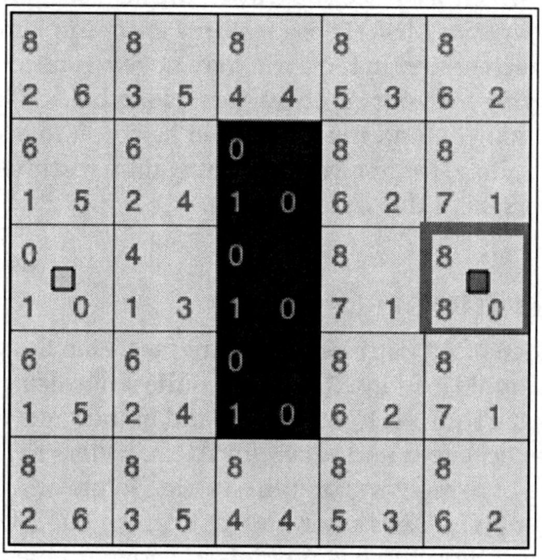

Reach target

Now all we have to do is to trace back starting from the target tile using its parent tile. This will give a path that looks something like the following figure:

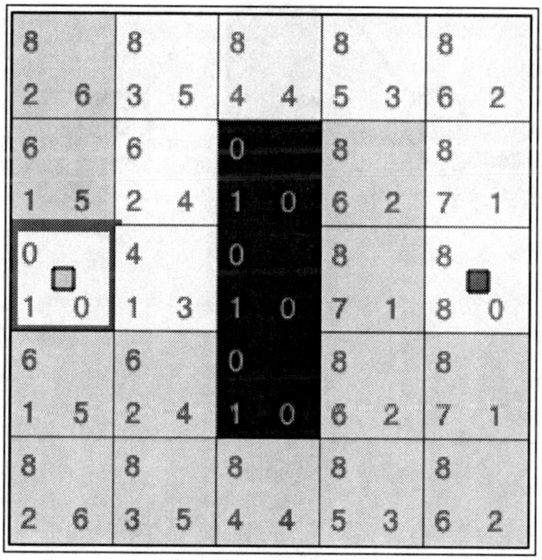

Path traced back

So this is the concept of A* pathfinding in a nutshell, without displaying any code. A* is an important concept in the AI pathfinding area, but since Unity 3.5, there are a couple of new features such as automatic navigation mesh generation and the Nav Mesh Agent, which we'll see roughly in the next section and then in more detail in *Chapter 8, Navigation Mesh*. These features make implementing pathfinding in your games very much easier. In fact, you may not even need to know about A* to implement pathfinding for your AI characters. Nonetheless, knowing how the system is actually working behind the scenes will help you to become a solid AI programmer. Unfortunately, those advanced navigation features in Unity are only available in the Pro version at this moment.

A navigation mesh

Now we have some idea of A* pathfinding techniques. One thing that you might notice is that using a simple grid in A* requires quite a number of computations to get a path which is the shortest to the target, and at the same time avoids the obstacles. So, to make it cheaper and easier for AI characters to find a path, people came up with the idea of using waypoints as a guide to move AI characters from the start point to the target point. Let's say we want to move our AI character from point A to point B, and we've set up three waypoints as shown in the following figure:

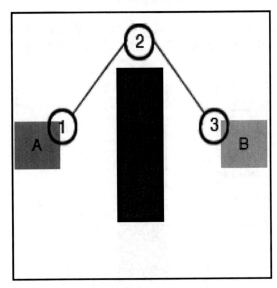

Waypoints

All we have to do now is to pick up the nearest waypoint, and then follow its connected node leading to the target waypoint. Most of the games use waypoints for pathfinding, because they are simple and quite effective in using less computation resources. However, they do have some issues. What if we want to update the obstacles in our map? We'll also have to place waypoints for the updated map again, as shown in the following figure:

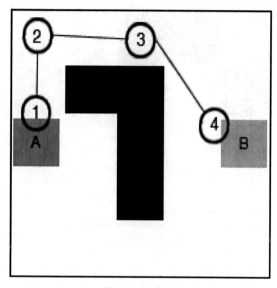

New waypoints

Following each node to the target can mean the AI character moves in zigzag directions. Look at the preceding figures; it's quite likely that the AI character will collide with the wall where the path is close to the wall. If that happens, our AI will keep trying to go through the wall to reach the next target, but it won't be able to and it will get stuck there. Even though we can smooth out the zigzag path by transforming it to a spline and do some adjustments to avoid such obstacles, the problem is the waypoints don't give any information about the environment, other than the spline connected between two nodes. What if our smoothed and adjusted path passes the edge of a cliff or a bridge? The new path might not be a safe path anymore. So, for our AI entities to be able to effectively traverse the whole level, we're going to need a tremendous number of waypoints, which will be really hard to implement and manage.

Let's look at a better solution, navigation mesh. A navigation mesh is another graph structure that can be used to represent our world, similar to the way we did with our square tile-based grid or waypoints graph.

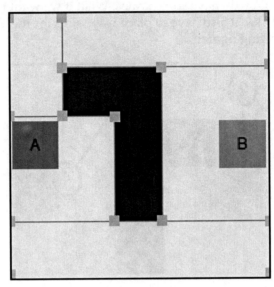

Navigation mesh

A navigation mesh uses convex polygons to represent the areas in the map that an AI entity can travel. The most important benefit of using a navigation mesh is that it gives a lot more information about the environment than a waypoint system. Now we can adjust our path safely, because we know the safe region in which our AI entities can travel. Another advantage of using a navigation mesh is that we can use the same mesh for different types of AI entities. Different AI entities can have different properties such as size, speed, and movement abilities. A set of waypoints is tailored for human, AI may not work nicely for flying creatures or AI controlled vehicles. Those might need different sets of waypoints. Using a navigation mesh can save a lot of time in such cases.

But generating a navigation mesh programmatically based on a scene, is a somewhat complicated process. Fortunately, Unity 3.5 introduced a built-in navigation mesh generator (Pro only feature). Since this is not a book on core AI techniques, we won't go too much into how to really generate and use such navigation meshes. Instead, we'll learn how to use Unity's navigation mesh for generating features to easily implement our AI pathfinding.

The behavior trees

Behavior trees are the other techniques used to represent and control the logic behind AI characters. They have become popular for the applications in AAA games such as Halo and Spore. Previously, we have briefly covered FSM. FSMs provide a very simple way to define the logic of an AI character, based on the different states and transitions between them. However, FSMs are considered difficult to scale and re-use existing logic. We need to add many states and hard-wire many transitions, in order to support all the scenarios, which we want our AI character to consider. So, we need a more scalable approach when dealing with large problems. behavior trees are a better way to implement AI game characters that could potentially become more and more complex.

The basic elements of behavior trees are tasks, where states are the main elements for FSMs. There are a few different tasks such as Sequence, Selector, and Parallel Decorator. This is quite confusing. The best way to understand this is to look at an example. Let's try to translate our example from the FSM section using a behavior tree. We can break all the transitions and states into tasks.

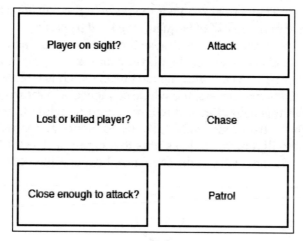

Tasks

Let's look at a Selector task for this Behavior tree. Selector tasks are represented with a circle and a question mark inside. First it'll choose to attack the player. If the Attack task returns success, the Selector task is done and will go back to the parent node, if there is one. If the Attack task fails, it'll try the Chase task. If the Chase task fails, it'll try the Patrol task.

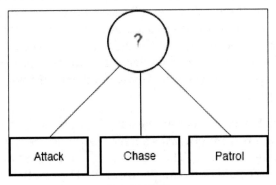

Selector task

What about the tests? They are also one of the tasks in the behavior trees. The following diagram shows the use of Sequence tasks, denoted by a rectangle with an arrow inside it. The root selector may choose the first Sequence action. This Sequence action's first task is to check whether the player character is close enough to attack. If this task succeeds, it'll proceed with the next task, which is to attack the player. If the Attack task also returns success, the whole sequence will return success, and the selector is done with this behavior, and will not continue with other Sequence tasks. If the Close enough to attack? task fails, then the Sequence action will not proceed to the Attack task, and will return a failed status to the parent selector task. Then the selector will choose the next task in the sequence, Lost or Killed Player?.

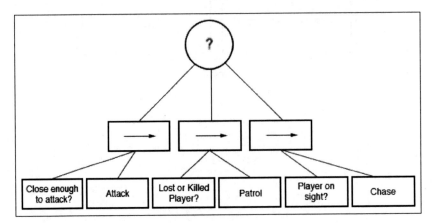

Sequence tasks

The other two common components are Parallel and Decorator. A Parallel task will execute all of its child tasks at the same time, while the Sequence and Selector tasks only execute their child tasks one by one. Decorator is another type of task that has only one child. It can change the behavior of its own child's tasks, which includes whether to run its child's task or not, how many times it should run, and so on.

We'll study how to implement a basic behavior tree system in Unity *Chapter 9, Behavior Trees*. There's a free add-on for Unity called Behave in the Unity Asset Store. Behave is a useful, free GUI editor to set up behavior trees of AI characters, and we'll look at it in more detail later as well.

Locomotion

Animals (including humans) have a very complex musculoskeletal system (the locomotor system) that gives them the ability to move around the body using the muscular and skeletal systems. We know where to put our steps when climbing a ladder, stairs, or on uneven terrain, and we know how to balance our body to stabilize all the fancy poses we want to make. We can do all this using our bones, muscles, joints, and other tissues, collectively described as our locomotor system.

Now put that into our game development perspective. Let's say we've a human character who needs to walk on both even and uneven surfaces, or on small slopes, and we have only one animation for a "walk" cycle. With the lack of a locomotor system in our virtual character, this is how it would look:

Climbing stair without locomotion

First we play the walk animation and advance the player forward. Now the character knows it's penetrating the surface. So, the collision detection system will pull the character up above the surface to prevent this penetration. This is how we usually set up the movement on an uneven surface. Even though it doesn't give a realistic look and feel, it does the job and is cheap to implement.

Let's take a look at how we really walk up stairs. We put our step firmly on the staircase, and using this force we pull up the rest of our body for the next step. This is how we do it in real life with our advanced locomotor system. However, it's not so simple to implement this level of realism inside games. We'll need a lot of animations for different scenarios, which include climbing ladders, walking/running up stairs, and so on. So, only the large studios with a lot of animators could pull this off in the past, until we came up with an automated system.

With a locomotion system

Fortunately, Unity 3D has an extension that can do just that, which is a locomotion system.

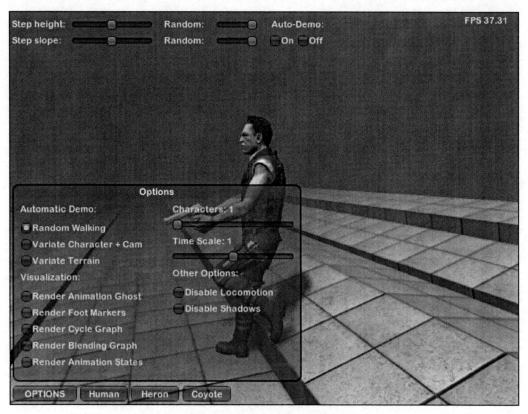

Locomotion system Unity extension

This system can automatically blend our animated walk/run cycles, and adjust the movements of the bones in the legs to ensure that the feet step correctly on the ground. It can also adjust the original animations made for a specific speed and direction on any surface, arbitrary steps, and slopes. We'll see how to use this locomotion system to apply realistic movement to our AI characters in a later chapter.

Dijkstra's algorithm

The Dijkstra's algorithm, named after professor *Edsger Dijkstra*, who devised the algorithm, is one of the most famous algorithms for finding the shortest paths in a graph with non-negative edge path costs. The algorithm was originally designed to solve the shortest path problem in the context of mathematical graph theory. And it's designed to find all the shortest paths from a starting node to all the other nodes in the graph. Since most of the games only need the shortest path between one starting point and one target point, all the other paths generated or found by this algorithm are not really useful. We can stop the algorithm, once we find the shortest path from a single starting point to a target point. But still it'll try to find all the shortest paths from all the points it has visited. So, this algorithm is not efficient enough to be used in most games. And we won't be doing a Unity demo of Dijkstra's algorithm in this book as well.

However, Dijkstra's algorithm is an important algorithm for the games that require strategic AI that needs as much information as possible about the map to make tactical decisions. It has many applications other than games, such as finding the shortest path in network routing protocols.

Summary

Game AI and academic AI have different objectives. Academic AI researches try to solve real-world problems, and prove a theory without much limited resources. Game AI focuses on building NPCs within limited resources that seems to be intelligent to the player. Objective of AI in games is to provide a challenging opponent that makes the game more fun to play with. We also learned briefly about the different AI techniques that are widely used in games such as finite state machines (FSMs), random and probability, sensor and input system, flocking and group behaviors, path following and steering behaviors, AI path finding, navigation mesh generation, and behavior trees. We'll see how to implement these techniques inside the Unity engine in the following chapters.

2
Finite State Machines

In this chapter, we'll learn how to use FSM in a Unity3D game, using a simple tank game mechanic example that comes with this book. We'll be dissecting the code and the components in this project.

In our game, the player will be able to control a tank. The enemy tanks will be moving around in the scene with reference to four waypoints. Once the player tank enters their visible range, they will start chasing us; and once they are close enough to attack, they'll start shooting at our player tank. Is this simple enough? We'll implement FSMs to control the AI of our enemy tank. First we'll use simple `switch` statements to implement our tank AI states, and then we'll use a FSM framework, which is based on and adapted from the C# FSM framework, and can be found at the following link:

http://wiki.unity3d.com/index.php?title=Finite_State_Machine

The player's tank

Now before writing the script for our player tank, let's take a look at how we set up the **PlayerTank** game object. Our **Tank** object is basically a simple **Mesh** with a **Rigidbody** component, and a **Box Collider** component. The **Tank** object is not a single **Mesh**, but two separate meshes, **Tank** and **Turret**. We make **Turret** a child of **Tank**. This is to allow independent rotation of the **Turret** object using the mouse movement. And at the same time, since it's the child of the **Tank** object, it'll follow wherever the **Tank** body goes as well. Then create an empty game object to be our **SpawnPoint** transform. It will be used as a reference position point, when shooting a bullet. Also we need to assign the **Player** tag to our **Tank** object. So that's how our **Tank** entity is set up. Now let's take a look at the controller class.

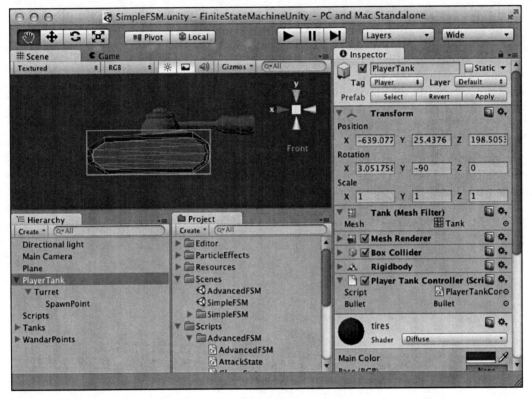

Tank entity

The PlayerTankController class

This class will be the primary means by which the player will control the **Tank** object using it. We will be using the *W*, *A*, *S*, and *D* keys to move and steer the tank, and the left mouse button to aim and shoot the **Turret** object.

Unity only knows how to work with the standard QWERTY keyboard layout. For those of us who use a different keyboard, all we have to do is pretend that we are using a QWERTY keyboard, and then everything will work out fine.

This book will also assume the use of a QWERTY keyboard, as well as the use of a two-button mouse, with the left mouse button set to the primary mouse button.

Initialization

The properties of our TankController class are as follows. First we set up our Start function and the Update functions.

The code in the PlayerTankController.cs file is as follows:

```
using UnityEngine;
using System.Collections;

public class PlayerTankController : MonoBehaviour
{
    public GameObject Bullet;

    private Transform Turret;
    private Transform bulletSpawnPoint;
    private float curSpeed, targetSpeed, rotSpeed;
    private float turretRotSpeed = 10.0f;
    private float maxForwardSpeed = 300.0f;
    private float maxBackwardSpeed = -300.0f;

    //Bullet shooting rate
    protected float shootRate = 0.5f;
    protected float elapsedTime;

    void Start()
    {

      //Tank Settings
      rotSpeed = 150.0f;

      //Get the turret of the tank
      Turret = gameObject.transform.GetChild(0).transform;
      bulletSpawnPoint = Turret.GetChild(0).transform;
    }
```

```
void Update()
{
  UpdateWeapon();
  UpdateControl();
}
```

The first child object of our `Tank` entity is the `Turret` object, and the first child of the `Turret` object is the `bulletSpawnPoint`. The `Start` function finds these objects, and then assigns them to their respective variables. We will assign our `Bullet` variable later, after we create our `Bullet` object. Also we included the `Update` function, which calls our `UpdateControl` and `UpdateWeapon` functions, which we will create soon.

Shooting bullet

Whenever the player clicks the left mouse button, we check whether the total elapsed time since the last fire has passed the fire rate of the weapon. If it has, then we create a new `Bullet` object at the `SpawnPoint` variable's position. This way, we can prevent shooting continuously without any limit.

```
void UpdateWeapon()
{
  if (Input.GetMouseButtonDown(0))
  {
    elapsedTime += Time.deltaTime;
    if (elapsedTime >= shootRate)
    {
      //Reset the time
      elapsedTime = 0.0f;

      //Instantiate the bullet
      Instantiate(Bullet, bulletSpawnPoint.position,
      bulletSpawnPoint.rotation);
    }
  }
}
```

Controlling the tank

The player will rotate the `Turret` object using the mouse. So, this part is a little bit tricky. Our `Camera` will look down upon the battlefield. From that, we'll use ray casting to determine the direction to turn, based on the `mousePosition` object on the battlefield.

```
void UpdateControl()
{
  //AIMING WITH THE MOUSE
  //Generate a plane that intersects the transform's
```

```
//position with an upwards normal.
Plane playerPlane = new Plane(Vector3.up,
transform.position + new Vector3(0, 0, 0));

// Generate a ray from the cursor position
Ray RayCast =
Camera.main.ScreenPointToRay(Input.mousePosition);

//Determine the point where the cursor ray intersects
//the plane.
float HitDist = 0;

// If the ray is parallel to the plane, Raycast will
//return false.
if (playerPlane.Raycast(RayCast, out HitDist))
{
  //Get the point along the ray that hits the
  //calculated distance.
  Vector3 RayHitPoint = RayCast.GetPoint(HitDist);

  Quaternion targetRotation =
  Quaternion.LookRotation(RayHitPoint -
  transform.position);

  Turret.transform.rotation =
  Quaternion.Slerp(Turret.transform.rotation,
  targetRotation, Time.deltaTime *
  turretRotSpeed);
}
```

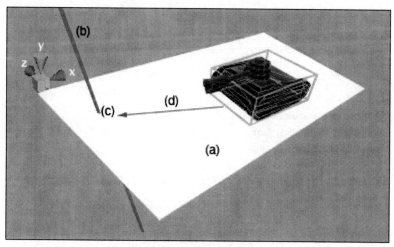

Raycast to aim with mouse

This is how it works:

1. Set up a plane that intersects with the player tank with an upward normal.
2. Shoot a ray from screen space with the mouse position (in the preceding diagram, it's assumed that we're looking down at the tank).
3. Find the point where the ray intersects the plane.
4. Finally, find the rotation from the current position to that intersection point.

Then we check for the key-pressed inputs, and then move/rotate the tank accordingly.

```
if (Input.GetKey(KeyCode.W))
{
  targetSpeed = maxForwardSpeed;
}
else if (Input.GetKey(KeyCode.S))
{
  targetSpeed = maxBackwardSpeed;
}
else
{
  targetSpeed = 0;
}

if (Input.GetKey(KeyCode.A))
{
  transform.Rotate(0, -rotSpeed * Time.deltaTime,
  0.0f);
}
else if (Input.GetKey(KeyCode.D))
{
  transform.Rotate(0, rotSpeed * Time.deltaTime,
  0.0f);
}

//Determine current speed
curSpeed = Mathf.Lerp(curSpeed, targetSpeed, 7.0f *
Time.deltaTime);

transform.Translate(Vector3.forward * Time.deltaTime *
curSpeed);
  }
}
```

The bullet class

Next our **Bullet** prefab is set up with two orthogonal planes using laser-like materials, and a **Particles/Additive** in the **Shader** field.

Bullet prefab

The code in the Bullet.cs file is as follows:

```
using UnityEngine;
using System.Collections;

public class Bullet : MonoBehaviour
{
    //Explosion Effect
    public GameObject Explosion;

    public float Speed = 600.0f;
    public float LifeTime = 3.0f;
    public int damage = 50;
```

```
void Start()
{
  Destroy(gameObject, LifeTime);
}

void Update()
{
  transform.position +=
  transform.forward * Speed * Time.deltaTime;
}

void OnCollisionEnter(Collision collision)
{
  ContactPoint contact = collision.contacts[0];
  Instantiate(Explosion, contact.point,
  Quaternion.identity);
  Destroy(gameObject);
}
}
```

We have three properties, damage, Speed, and Lifetime for our bullet, so that the bullet will be automatically destroyed after its lifetime.

You can see the **Explosion** property of the bullet is linked to the **ParticleExplosion** prefab, which we're not going to discuss in detail. There's a prefab called **ParticleExplosion** under the ParticleEffects folder. We just drop that prefab into this field. This particle effect is played when the bullet is hit with something as described in the OnCollisionEnter method. This **ParticleExplosion** prefab uses a script called AutoDestruct to destroy the Explosion object automatically after a certain amount of time.

Downloading the example code

You can download the example code files for all Packt books you have purchased from your account at http://www.packtpub.com. If you purchased this book elsewhere, you can visit http://www.packtpub.com/support and register to have the files e-mailed directly to you.

Setting up waypoints

Next, we put four **Cube** game objects at random places, as the waypoints inside our scene, and name them **WandarPoints**.

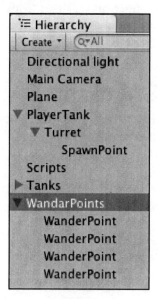

WanderPoints

Here is what our WanderPoint object will look like:.

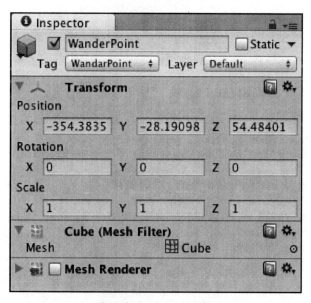

WanderPoint properties

One thing to note here is the need to tag those points with a tag called **WandarPoint**. We'll be referencing this tag, when we try to find the waypoints from our tank AI. As you can see in its properties, a waypoint here is just a **Cube** game object with the **Mesh Renderer** checkbox disabled, and the **Box Collider** object removed. We can even use an empty game object, since all we need from a waypoint is its position and the transformation data. But we're using the **Cube** objects here, so that we can visualize the waypoints if we want to.

The abstract FSM class

Next, we'll implement a generic abstract class that defines the methods which our enemy tank AI class has to implement.

The code in the FSM.cs file is as follows:

```
using UnityEngine;
using System.Collections;

public class FSM : MonoBehaviour
{
    //Player Transform
    protected Transform playerTransform;

    //Next destination position of the NPC Tank
    protected Vector3 destPos;

    //List of points for patrolling
    protected GameObject[] pointList;

    //Bullet shooting rate
    protected float shootRate;
    protected float elapsedTime;

    //Tank Turret
    public Transform turret { get; set; }
    public Transform bulletSpawnPoint { get; set; }

    protected virtual void Initialize() { }
    protected virtual void FSMUpdate() { }
    protected virtual void FSMFixedUpdate() { }

    // Use this for initialization
    void Start ()
    {
```

```
        Initialize();
    }

    // Update is called once per frame
    void Update ()
    {
        FSMUpdate();
    }

    void FixedUpdate()
    {
        FSMFixedUpdate();
    }
}
```

All that the enemy tanks need to know is the position of player tank, their next destination point, and the list of waypoints to choose, while they're patrolling. Once the player tank is in range, they will rotate their `turret` object and then start shooting from the bullet spawn point at their fire rate.

The inherited classes will also need to implement the three methods: `Initialize`, `FSMUpdate`, and `FSMFixedUpdate`. So, this is the abstract class, which our tank AI will be implementing.

The enemy tank AI

Now let's look at the real code for our AI tanks. Let's call our class `SimpleFSM`, which inherits from our `FSM` abstract class.

The code in the `SimpleFSM.cs` file is as follows:

```
using UnityEngine;
using System.Collections;

public class SimpleFSM : FSM
{

    public enum FSMState
    {
        None,
        Patrol,
        Chase,
        Attack,
        Dead,
    }
```

```
//Current state that the NPC is reaching
public FSMState curState;

//Speed of the tank
private float curSpeed;

//Tank Rotation Speed
private float curRotSpeed;

//Bullet
public GameObject Bullet;

//Whether the NPC is destroyed or not
private bool bDead;
private int health;
```

Here, we are declaring a few variables. Our tank AI will have four different states: Patrol, Chase, Attack, and Dead. Basically, we'll be implementing the FSM that was described as an example in *Chapter 1, Introduction to AI*.

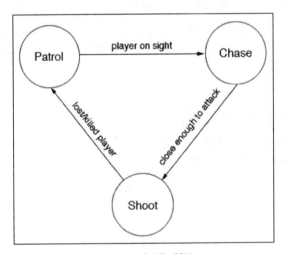

Enemy tank AI's FSM

In our Initialize method, we set up our AI tank's properties with default values. Then we store the positions of waypoints in our local variable. We got those waypoints from our scene using the FindGameObjectsWithTag method, trying to find those objects with the WandarPoint tag.

```
//Initialize the Finite state machine for the NPC tank
protected override void Initialize ()
{
    curState = FSMState.Patrol;
    curSpeed = 150.0f;
    curRotSpeed = 2.0f;
```

```
bDead = false;
elapsedTime = 0.0f;
shootRate = 3.0f;
health = 100;

//Get the list of points
pointList =
GameObject.FindGameObjectsWithTag("WandarPoint");

//Set Random destination point first
FindNextPoint();

//Get the target enemy(Player)
GameObject objPlayer =
GameObject.FindGameObjectWithTag("Player");

playerTransform = objPlayer.transform;

if (!playerTransform)
  print("Player doesn't exist.. Please add one "+
  "with Tag named 'Player'");

  //Get the turret of the tank
  turret = gameObject.transform.GetChild(0).transform;
  bulletSpawnPoint = turret.GetChild(0).transform;
}
```

Our update method that gets called every frame looks as follows:

```
//Update each frame
protected override void FSMUpdate()
{
  switch (curState)
  {
    case FSMState.Patrol: UpdatePatrolState(); break;
    case FSMState.Chase: UpdateChaseState(); break;
    case FSMState.Attack: UpdateAttackState(); break;
    case FSMState.Dead: UpdateDeadState(); break;
  }

  //Update the time
  elapsedTime += Time.deltaTime;

  //Go to dead state is no health left
  if (health <= 0)
   curState = FSMState.Dead;
}
```

We check the current state, and then call the appropriate state method. Once the health object is zero or less than zero, we set the tank to the Dead state.

The patrol state

While our tank is in the `Patrol` state, we check whether it has reached the destination point. If it has, it'll find the next destination point to follow. The `FindNextPoint` method basically chooses the next random destination point among the waypoints defined. If it's still on the way to the current destination point, it'll check the distance with the player's tank. If the player's tank is in range (which is `300` here), then it'll change to the `Chase` state. The rest of the code just rotates the tank and moves forward.

```
protected void UpdatePatrolState()
{
  //Find another random patrol point if the current
  //point is reached
  if (Vector3.Distance(transform.position, destPos) <=
  100.0f)
  {
    print("Reached to the destination point\n"+
    "calculating the next point");

    FindNextPoint();
  }

  //Check the distance with player tank
  //When the distance is near, transition to chase state
  else if (Vector3.Distance(transform.position,
  playerTransform.position) <= 300.0f)
  {
    print("Switch to Chase Position");
    curState = FSMState.Chase;
  }

  //Rotate to the target point
  Quaternion targetRotation =
  Quaternion.LookRotation(destPos
  - transform.position);

  transform.rotation =
  Quaternion.Slerp(transform.rotation,
  targetRotation, Time.deltaTime * curRotSpeed);

  //Go Forward
  transform.Translate(Vector3.forward * Time.deltaTime *
  curSpeed);
}
protected void FindNextPoint()
{
```

```
print("Finding next point");
int rndIndex = Random.Range(0, pointList.Length);
float rndRadius = 10.0f;
Vector3 rndPosition = Vector3.zero;
destPos = pointList[rndIndex].transform.position +
rndPosition;

//Check Range to decide the random point
//as the same as before
if (IsInCurrentRange(destPos))
{
  rndPosition = new Vector3(Random.Range(-rndRadius,
  rndRadius), 0.0f, Random.Range(-rndRadius,
  rndRadius));
  destPos = pointList[rndIndex].transform.position +
  rndPosition;
}
}
protected bool IsInCurrentRange(Vector3 pos)
{
  float xPos = Mathf.Abs(pos.x - transform.position.x);
  float zPos = Mathf.Abs(pos.z - transform.position.z);

  if (xPos <= 50 && zPos <= 50)
    return true;

    return false;
}
```

The chase state

Similarly while the tank is in the Chase state, it'll check its distance with the player tank. If it's close enough, it'll switch to the Attack state. If the player tank has gone too far, then it'll go back to the Patrol state.

```
protected void UpdateChaseState()
{
  //Set the target position as the player position
  destPos = playerTransform.position;

  //Check the distance with player tank When
  //the distance is near, transition to attack state
  float dist = Vector3.Distance(transform.position,
  playerTransform.position);
```

```
       if (dist <= 200.0f)
       {
          curState = FSMState.Attack;
       }
       //Go back to patrol is it become too far
       else if (dist >= 300.0f)
       {
          curState = FSMState.Patrol;
       }

       //Go Forward
       transform.Translate(Vector3.forward * Time.deltaTime *
       curSpeed);
}
```

The attack state

If the player tank is close enough to attack our AI tank, we will rotate the turret object to the player tank, and then start shooting. It'll go back to the Patrol state, if the player tank is out of range.

```
protected void UpdateAttackState()
{
   //Set the target position as the player position
   destPos = playerTransform.position;

   //Check the distance with the player tank
   float dist = Vector3.Distance(transform.position,
   playerTransform.position);

   if (dist >= 200.0f && dist < 300.0f)
   {
      //Rotate to the target point
      Quaternion targetRotation =
      Quaternion.LookRotation(destPos -
      transform.position);
      transform.rotation = Quaternion.Slerp(
      transform.rotation, targetRotation,
      Time.deltaTime * curRotSpeed);

      //Go Forward
      transform.Translate(Vector3.forward *
      Time.deltaTime * curSpeed);
```

```
      curState = FSMState.Attack;
   }
   //Transition to patrol is the tank become too far
   else if (dist >= 300.0f)
   {
      curState = FSMState.Patrol;
   }

   //Always Turn the turret towards the player
   Quaternion turretRotation =
   Quaternion.LookRotation(destPos
   - turret.position);

   turret.rotation =
   Quaternion.Slerp(turret.rotation, turretRotation,
   Time.deltaTime * curRotSpeed);

   //Shoot the bullets
   ShootBullet();
}
private void ShootBullet()
{
   if (elapsedTime >= shootRate)
   {
      //Shoot the bullet
      Instantiate(Bullet, bulletSpawnPoint.position,
      bulletSpawnPoint.rotation);
      elapsedTime = 0.0f;
   }
}
```

The dead state

If the tank has reached the Dead state, we'll have it explode.

```
protected void UpdateDeadState()
{
   //Show the dead animation with some physics effects
   if (!bDead)
   {
      bDead = true;
      Explode();
   }
}
```

Here's a small function that will give a nice explosion effect. We just apply an `ExplosionForce` to our `rigidbody` component with some random directions, given in the following code:

```
protected void Explode()
{
  float rndX = Random.Range(10.0f, 30.0f);
  float rndZ = Random.Range(10.0f, 30.0f);
  for (int i = 0; i < 3; i++)
  {
    rigidbody.AddExplosionForce(10000.0f,
    transform.position - new Vector3(rndX, 10.0f,
    rndZ), 40.0f, 10.0f);
    rigidbody.velocity = transform.TransformDirection(
    new Vector3(rndX, 20.0f, rndZ));
  }

  Destroy(gameObject, 1.5f);
}
```

Taking damage

If the tank is hit by a bullet, then the `health` property's value will be deducted, based on the **Bullet** object's `damage` value.

```
void OnCollisionEnter(Collision collision)
{
  //Reduce health
  if(collision.gameObject.tag == "Bullet")
  {
    health -=collision.gameObject.GetComponent
    <Bullet>().damage;
  }
}
```

You can open `SimpleFSM.scene` in Unity, and then you should see the AI tanks patrolling, chasing, and attacking the player. Our player tank doesn't take damage from AI tanks, so it'll never get destroyed. But AI tanks have the `health` property, and take damage from the player's bullets. So, you'll see their explosion, once their `health` property reaches zero.

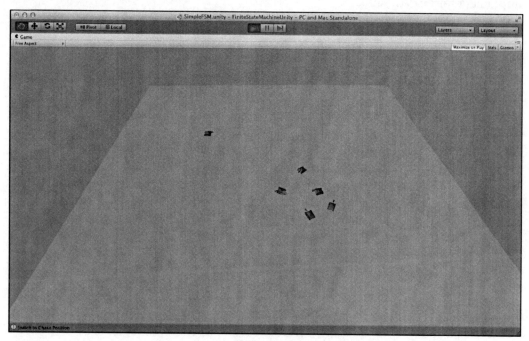

AI tanks in action

Using an FSM framework

The FSM framework we're going to use here is adapted from the C# FSM framework, which can be found at `unifycommunity.com`. That framework is again a part of the Deterministic Finite State Machine framework, based on *Chapter 3.1* of *Game Programming Gems 1*, by *Eric Dybsend*. We'll only be looking at the differences between this FSM and the one we made earlier. The complete FSM can be found with the assets that come with the book. We'll now study how the framework works and how to use it to implement our tank AI.

The `AdvanceFSM` and the `FSMState` are the two main classes of our framework. Let's take a look at them.

The AdvanceFSM class

The AdvanceFSM class basically manages all the FSMState(s) implemented, and keeps updated with the transitions and the current state. So, the first thing to do before using our framework is to declare the transitions and states that we plan to implement for our AI tanks.

The code in the AdvancedFSM.cs file is as follows:

```
using UnityEngine;
using System.Collections;
using System.Collections.Generic;

public enum Transition
{
    None = 0,
    SawPlayer,
    ReachPlayer,
    LostPlayer,
    NoHealth,
}

public enum FSMStateID
{
    None = 0,
    Patrolling,
    Chasing,
    Attacking,
    Dead,
}
```

It has a list object to store the FSMState objects, and two local variables to store the current ID of the FSMState class, and current FSMState itself.

```
private List<FSMState> fsmStates;
    private FSMStateID currentStateID;
    public FSMStateID CurrentStateID
    {
      get
      {
        return currentStateID;
      }
    }
```

```
    private FSMState currentState;
    public FSMState CurrentState
    {
      get
      {
        return currentState;
      }
    }
```

The `AddFSMState` and the `DeleteState` methods add and delete the instances of our `FSMState` class in our list respectively. When the `PerformTransition` method is called, it updates the `CurrentState` variable with the new state based on the transition.

The FSMState class

`FSMState` manages the transitions to other states. It has a dictionary object called `map` to store the key-value pairs of transitions and states. For example, the `SawPlayer` transition maps to the `Chasing` state, and `LostPlayer` maps to the `Patrolling` state, and so on.

The code in the `FSMState.cs` file is as follows:

```
using UnityEngine;
using System.Collections;
using System.Collections.Generic;

public abstract class FSMState
{
    protected Dictionary<Transition, FSMStateID> map = new
    Dictionary<Transition, FSMStateID>();
...
```

The `AddTransition` and the `DeleteTransition` methods simply add and delete transitions from its state-transition dictionary `map` object. The `GetOutputState` method looks up from the `map` object, and returns the state based on the input transition.

The `FSMState` class also declares two abstract methods that its child classes need to implement. They are as follows:

```
...
public abstract void Reason(Transform player, Transform npc);
public abstract void Act(Transform player, Transform npc);
...
```

The Reason method has to check whether the state should do the transition to another state. And the Act method does the actual execution of the tasks for the currentState variable such as moving towards a destination point, and then chasing or attacking the player. Both methods require transformed data of the player and the NPC entity, which can be obtained using this class.

The state classes

Unlike in our previous SimpleFSM example, the states for our tank AI are written in separate classes inherited from the FSMState class as AttackState, ChaseState, DeadState, and PatrolState, each of which implements the Reason and Act methods. Let's take a look at the PatrolState class as an example.

The PatrolState class

It has three methods: a constructor, a Reason, and an Act.

The code in the PatrolState.cs file is as follows:

```
using UnityEngine;
using System.Collections;

public class PatrolState : FSMState
{

    public PatrolState(Transform[] wp)
    {
      waypoints = wp;
      stateID = FSMStateID.Patrolling;

      curRotSpeed = 1.0f;
      curSpeed = 100.0f;
    }

    public override void Reason(Transform player,
    Transform npc)
    {
      //Check the distance with player tank
      //When the distance is near, transition to chase state
      if (Vector3.Distance(npc.position, player.position) <=
      300.0f)
      {
        Debug.Log("Switch to Chase State");
```

```
      npc.GetComponent
      <NPCTankController>().SetTransition(
      Transition.SawPlayer);
    }
  }

  public override void Act(Transform player, Transform npc)
  {
    //Find another random patrol point if the current
    //point is reached

    if (Vector3.Distance(npc.position, destPos) <= 100.0f)
    {
      Debug.Log("Reached to the destination" +
      point\ncalculating the next point");
      FindNextPoint();
    }

    //Rotate to the target point
    Quaternion targetRotation =
    Quaternion.LookRotation(destPos - npc.position);

    npc.rotation = Quaternion.Slerp(npc.rotation,
    targetRotation, Time.deltaTime * curRotSpeed);

    //Go Forward
    npc.Translate(Vector3.forward *
    Time.deltaTime * curSpeed);
  }
}
```

The constructor method takes the `waypoints` array and stores them in a local array, and then it initializes properties such as movement and rotation speed. The `Reason` method checks the distance between itself (the AI tank) and the player tank. If the player tank is in range, it sets the transition ID to the `SawPlayer` transition using the `SetTransition` method of the `NPCTankController` class, which looks as follows:

The code in the `NPCTankController.cs` file is as follows:

```
public void SetTransition(Transition t)
{
    PerformTransition(t);
}
```

It's just a wrapper method that calls the `PerformTransition` method of the `AdvanceFSM` class. This method will update the `CurrentState` variable, with the one responsible for this transition, using the `Transition` object, and the state-transition dictionary `map` object from the `FSMState` class. The `Act` method simply updates the AI tank's destination point, rotates the tank in that direction, and then moves forward. Other state classes also follow this template with different reasoning and acting procedures. We've already seen them in our previous simple FSM examples, so we won't describe them here again. See if you can figure out how to set these classes up on your own. If you get stuck, the assets that come with this book will have the code for you to look at.

The NPCTankController class

Our tank AI, the `NPCTankController` class will inherit from `AdvanceFSM`. This is how we set up the states for our NPC tanks:

```
...
    private void ConstructFSM()
    {


        PatrolState patrol = new PatrolState(waypoints);
        patrol.AddTransition(Transition.SawPlayer,
        FSMStateID.Chasing);
        patrol.AddTransition(Transition.NoHealth,
        FSMStateID.Dead);

        ChaseState chase = new ChaseState(waypoints);
        chase.AddTransition(Transition.LostPlayer,
        FSMStateID.Patrolling);
        chase.AddTransition(Transition.ReachPlayer,
        FSMStateID.Attacking);
        chase.AddTransition(Transition.NoHealth,
        FSMStateID.Dead);

        AttackState attack = new AttackState(waypoints);
        attack.AddTransition(Transition.LostPlayer,
        FSMStateID.Patrolling);
        attack.AddTransition(Transition.SawPlayer,
        FSMStateID.Chasing);
        attack.AddTransition(Transition.NoHealth,
        FSMStateID.Dead);
```

```
DeadState dead = new DeadState();
dead.AddTransition(Transition.NoHealth,
FSMStateID.Dead);

AddFSMState(patrol);
AddFSMState(chase);
AddFSMState(attack);
AddFSMState(dead);
}
```

Here's the beauty of using our FSM framework. Since the states are self-managed within their respective classes, our NPCTankController class only needs to call the Reason and Act methods of the current active state. This eliminates the need to write a long list of the if/else and switch statements, and bloated code. Instead, now our states are nicely packaged in the classes of their own, making the code more manageable as the number of states to implement, and the transitions between them become more and more complex in bigger projects.

. . .

```
protected override void FSMFixedUpdate()
{
  CurrentState.Reason(playerTransform, transform);
  CurrentState.Act(playerTransform, transform);
}
```

So, this is how our framework works. In summary, the main steps to use this framework are as follows:

1. Declare transitions and states in the AdvanceFSM class.
2. Write the state classes inherited from the FSMState class, and then implement the Reason and Act methods.
3. Write the custom NPC AI class inherited from AdvanceFSM.
4. Create states from the state classes, and then add transition and state pairs using the AddTransition method of the FSMState class.
5. Add those states into the state list of the AdvanceFSM class, using the AddFSMState method.
6. Call the CurrentState variable's Reason and Act methods in the game update cycle.

You can play around with the AdvancedFSM.scene in Unity. It'll run in the same way as our previous SimpleFSM example. But now the code and classes are more organized and manageable.

Summary

In this chapter, we learned how to implement state machines in Unity3D based on a simple tank game. We first looked at how to implement FSM in the simplest way, using the `switch` statements. Then we studied how to use a framework to make the AI implementation easier to manage and extend.

In the next chapter, we will take a look at randomness and probability and how we can use it to make the outcome of our games more unpredictable.

3
Random and Probability

In this chapter, we are going to look at how the concepts of probability can be applied to game AI. This chapter will be more about generic game AI development techniques in random and probability topics, and less about Unity3D in particular. Moreover, they can be applied to any game development middleware or technology framework. We'll be using mono C# in Unity3D for the demos mainly using the console to output data, and won't address much about the specific features of the Unity3D engine and the editor itself.

Game developers use probability or the confidence factor to add a little uncertainty to the behaviors of AI characters, as well as to the game world. This makes the artificial intelligence system a bit unpredictable of a certain outcome, and can provide the players with a more exciting and challenging experience.

Let us take an example of a typical soccer game. One of the rules of a soccer game is to award a direct free kick if one player is fouled while trying to possess the ball from the opposing team. Now, instead of giving a foul and a free kick all the time whenever that foul happens, the game developer can apply a probability so that only 98 percent of all the fouls will be rewarded with a direct free kick. As a result, most of the time, the player will get a direct free kick. But when that remaining two percent happens, like you have hit the other player and you know it's going to be a free kick but the referee passes it, it can provide a certain emotional feedback to the players from both the teams (assuming that you are playing against another human). The other player would feel angry and disappointed, while you'd feel lucky and satisfied. In the end, the referees are human, and like all other humans, they might not be 100 percent correct all the time.

So we use probability in a game AI to make the game and characters livelier and seem more realistic, by not making the same decision or taking the same action again and again. There are many topics to discuss and debate in the probability domain. So this small single chapter will only be able to address the basic concepts, and how we can implement some of them in Unity3D.

In this chapter, we will be going over random and probability. We will be creating a simple dice game. We will also give some application examples of probability and dynamic AI. Finally, we will finish the chapter with a simple slot machine, and then add on more probability features.

Random

Probability is basically a measure of how likely it is that a particular condition or a favorable outcome can be achieved among all the possible outcomes, if selected randomly. So speaking of probability, one can't neglect the importance of randomness. **Random number generation** (RNG) is very important when we need to produce unpredictable results. The simplest and probably the oldest technique would be throwing a dice to generate a random value between one and six. The random numbers are produced computationally by a **pseudorandom number generator** (PRNG), and they determine the same sequence of random numbers based on the initial seed value. So, if we theoretically know the seed value, we can regenerate the same sequence of random numbers again, and thus they are not considered as truly random. The seed value is usually generated from the state of the computer system, such as the elapsed time in milliseconds since the computer starts running. Some RNGs are more random than others. If we were creating an encryption program, we would want to look into a more random RNG. For the games we will be making, the RNG that comes with Unity will suffice. Now let's see how we can generate random numbers in Unity3D.

Random class

The Unity3D script has a Random class to generate random data. Two of the most widely used properties would be seed and value:

```
static var seed : int
```

You can set this seed property of the Random class to seed the random number generator. Usually, we will not want to seed the same value again and again, as this will result in the same predictable sequence of random numbers being generated. One of the reasons for keeping the same seed value is for testing purposes:

```
static var value : float
```

You can read the Random.value property to get a random number between 0.0 (inclusive) and 1.0 (inclusive). Both 0.0 and 1.0 may be returned by this property. Another class method that could be quite handy is the Range method.

```
static function Range (min : float, max : float) : float
```

The `Range` method can be used to generate a random number from a range. When given an `integer value`, it returns a random `integer` number between `min` (inclusive) and `max` (exclusive). This means that a zero may be returned, but never a one. If you pass in float values for the range, it'll return a random `float` number between `min` (inclusive) and `max` (inclusive). Take note of the exclusive and inclusive parts. Since the `integer` random value is exclusive of `max` in range, we'll need to pass in `n+1` as the `max` range, where `n` is our desired maximum random integer. However, for the `float` random value, the max value in range is inclusive.

Simple random dice game

Let's set up a very simple dice game in a new scene, where a random number is being generated between one and six, and checked against the input value. The player will win, if the input value matches the dice result generated randomly as shown in the following `DiceGame.cs` file:.

```
using UnityEngine;
using System.Collections;

public class DiceGame : MonoBehaviour {

    public string inputValue = "1";

    void OnGUI() {
        GUI.Label(new Rect (10, 10, 100, 20), "Input: ");
        inputValue = GUI.TextField(new Rect(120, 10, 50, 20),
            inputValue, 25);
        if (GUI.Button(new Rect(100,50,50,30),"Play")) {
            Debug.Log("Throwing dice...");
            Debug.Log("Finding random between 1 to 6...");
            int diceResult = Random.Range(1,7);
            Debug.Log("Result: " + diceResult);
        if (diceResult == int.Parse(inputValue)) {
            guiText.text = "DICE RESULT: " +
                diceResult.ToString() + "\r\nYOU WIN!";
            }
        else {
            guiText.text = "DICE RESULT: " +
                diceResult.ToString() + "\r\nYOU LOSE!";
            }
        }
    }
}
```

We implement this simple dice game in the OnGUI() method as we want to render some GUI controls such as a label, a text field to enter the input value, and a button to play. The guiText object will be used to display the result. Add a guiText to the scene, navigate to **Game Object | Create Other | GUI Text**, and add our script to the object. The output that you get if you run the game is shown in the following screenshot:

Simple dice game results

This is a purely random game, and there's no modified probability involved. Each side of the surface of the dice has an equal chance to be picked.

Definition of probability

There are many ways to define probability based on the situations and the domain context. The most commonly used notion of probability is to refer the possibility of an event to successfully occur. The probability of an event A to occur is usually written as P(A). To calculate P(A) we need to know the number of ways or times it can occur (n), and the total number of times all the other possible events can occur (N).

So the probability of an event A can be calculated as

$$P(A) = n / N$$

P(A) is the probability of the event A to occur, and it's equal to the number of ways that A can occur (n) out of the number of all outcomes (N). If P(A) is the probability of the event A to successfully occur, then the probability of the event A will not occur, or the probability of failure for event A is equal to:

$$Pf (A) = 1 - P.(A)$$

The range of probability is a decimal number from zero to one. Probability of zero means there's no chance for the desired event to occur, and one means that it's 100 percent certain for the event to occur. And P(A) + Pf (A) must equal to one. Since the probability values range from zero to one, we can get the percentage value by multiplying by 100.

Independent and related events

Another important concept in probability is whether the chance of a particular event to occur depends on any other event in some ways or not. For example, throwing a six-sided dice twice are two independent events. Each time you throw a dice, the probability of each side to turn up is one-sixth. On the other hand, drawing two cards from the same deck are two related events. If you drew a Jack in the first event, there's one less chance that you can get another Jack in the second event.

Conditional probability

When throwing two six-sided dices at the same time, what is the probability of getting a one on both the dices? Here there are two conditional events; to get one on the first dice, and also to get one on the second dice. They rely on each other to calculate the probability of getting one on both the dices. The probability to get one on the first dice is one-sixth, and also for the second dice is one-sixth. So the answer would be one-sixth times one-sixth which is 1/36, or a 2.8 percent chance.

Now let's consider another example, what's the probability that the sum of the numbers show up on two dices is equal to two? Since there's only one way to get this sum, which is one and one, the probability is still the same as getting the same number on both dices. In that case it would be still 1/36.

But how about getting the sum of the numbers that show up on the two dices to seven? As you can see, there are a total of six possible chances to get a total of seven, from the following table:

Dice 1	Dice 2
1	6
2	5
3	4
4	3
5	2
6	1

So the probability of getting a sum of seven from two dices is 6/36 or one-sixth, which is 16.7 percent. These are some examples of conditional probability, where two events rely on each other to achieve a desirable outcome.

A loaded dice

Now let's assume we haven't been that honest, and our dice is loaded so that the side of the number six has a double chance of landing facing upward. For a six-sided dice, the probability of each side facing upward is approximately one-sixth (0.17). Since we doubled the chance of getting six, we need to double the probability of getting six, let's say up to 0.34. And the probability of the remaining five sides will be reduced to 0.132.

The simplest way to implement this loaded dice algorithm is to generate a random value between 1 and 100. Check if the random value is in a range of one to 35. If so return 6, otherwise get a random dice value between one and five, since these values have the same probability of 0.13.

So here's our throwLoadedDice() method:

```
int throwDiceLoaded() {
  Debug.Log("Throwing dice...");
    int randomProbability = Random.Range(1,101);
    int diceResult = 0;
    if (randomProbability < 36) {
      diceResult = 6;
    }
    else {
      diceResult = Random.Range(1,5);
    }
  Debug.Log("Result: " + diceResult);
    return diceResult;
}
```

If we test our new loaded dice algorithm by throwing the dice multiple times, you'll notice that the value 6 yields more than usual. Here is our new OnGUI() function:

```
void OnGUI() {
  GUI.Label(new Rect (10, 10, 50, 20), "Input: ");
  inputValue = GUI.TextField(new Rect(60, 10, 50, 20),
    inputValue, 25);
    if (GUI.Button(new Rect(60,40,50,30),"Play")) {
      int totalSix = 0;
        for (int i=0;i<10;i++) {
          int diceResult = throwDiceLoaded();
          if (diceResult == 6) totalSix++;
          if (diceResult == int.Parse(inputValue)) {
            guiText.text = "DICE RESULT: " +
              diceResult.ToString()+"\r\nYOU WIN!";
          }
```

```
    else {
      guiText.text = "DICE RESULT: " +
        diceResult.ToString()+"\r\nYOU LOSE!";
          }
        }
      Debug.Log("Total of six: " + totalSix.ToString());
    }
  }
```

We throw the dice ten times in our `OnGUI()` method, and here I got 6 at least two to three times (which is approximately 33 percent of ten times). But, if you normally throw the dice without any loaded probability it's more possible that you won't get any 6 at all. Keep in mind that the value 6 is only favored for 35 percent, and thus there's still a chance that you will never get a 6 out of ten dice throws, though it's quite unlikely.

Character personalities

We can also use different probabilities to specify the in-game characters' specialties. Let's pretend we designed a game proposal for a population management game for the local government. We need to address and simulate issues like taxation versus global talent attraction, immigration versus social cohesion, and so on. We have three types of characters in our proposal, namely, workers, scientists, and professionals. Their efficiencies in performing the particular tasks are defined in the following table:

Characters	Construction	R&D	Corporate Jobs
Worker	95	2	3
Scientist	5	85	10
Professional	10	10	80

Let us take a look at how we can implement this mechanic. Let's say the player needs to build new houses to accommodate the increased population. A house construction would require 1,000 units of workload to finish. We use the value specified earlier as the workload that can be done per second per unit type for a particular task. So if you're building a house with one worker that will only take about 10 seconds to finish the construction (`1000/95`) whereas it'll take more than three minutes if you are trying to build with the scientists (`1000/5 = 200 seconds`). The same will be true for other tasks such as R&D and corporate jobs. These factors can be adjusted/enhanced later as the game progresses, making some of the early level tasks become simpler, and takes less time.

Then we introduce special items that could be discovered by the particular unit type. Now, we don't want to give these items every time a particular unit has done its tasks. Instead we want to reward the player as a surprise. So we associate the probability of finding such items according to the unit type, as described in the following table:

Special items	Worker	Scientist	Professional
Raw materials	0.3	0.1	0.0
New tech	0.0	0.3	0.0
Bonus	0.1	0.2	0.4

The preceding table means there's a 30 percent chance that a worker will find some raw materials, and a 10 percent chance to earn bonus income whenever they have built a factory or a house. This allows the players to anticipate the possible upcoming rewards, once they've done some tasks. This can make the game more fun because the players will not know the outcome of the event.

FSM with probability

We discussed Finite State Machines (FSM) in *Chapter 2, Finite State Machines*, using both simple switch statements as well as using the FSM framework. The decision to choose which state to execute was purely based on true or false value of a given condition. Remember the following FSM of our AI controlled tank entity?

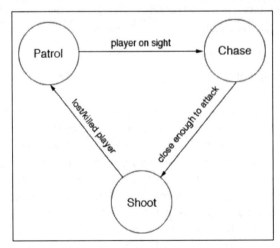

Tank AI FSM

To make the AI more interesting, and a little bit unpredictable, we can give our tank entity some options with probabilities to choose from, instead of doing the same thing whenever a certain condition is met. For example, in our earlier FSM, our AI tank will chase the player tank once the player is in its line of sight. Instead we can give our AI another state, such as flee with some probability such as 50 percent as shown in the following figure:

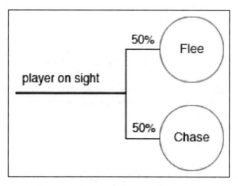

FSM using probability

Now instead of chasing every time, the AI tank spots the player; there's a 50 percent chance that it'll flee, and maybe report to the headquarters or something. We can implement this mechanic the same way we did with our previous dice example. First we need to generate a random value between one and 100, and see if the value lies between one and 50 or 51 and 100. (Or we could randomly choose between zero and one.) Then choose a state accordingly. The other way to implement this is to fill an array with these options in proportion to their respective probabilities. Then pick a random state from this pool as if you were drawing a lottery winner. Let's see how to use this technique as shown in the following FSM.cs file:

```
using UnityEngine;
using System.Collections;

public class FSM : MonoBehaviour {
  public enum FSMState {
    Chase,
    Flee
  }

  public int chaseProbabiilty = 50;
  public int fleeProbabiilty = 50;

  //a poll to store the states according to their
    //probabilities
  public ArrayList statesPoll = new ArrayList();
```

```
void Start () {
  //fill the array
    for (int i = 0; i < chaseProbabiilty; i++) {
      statesPoll.Add(FSMState.Chase);
    }
    for (int i = 0; i < fleeProbabiilty; i++) {
      statesPoll.Add(FSMState.Flee);
    }
  }

void OnGUI() {
    if (GUI.Button(new Rect(10,10,150,40),
      "Player on sight")) {
      int randomState = Random.Range(0, statesPoll.Count);
      Debug.Log(statesPoll[randomState].ToString());
    }
  }
}
```

In our OnGUI() method, when you click on the mouse button, we just choose one random item from our statesPoll array. Obviously, the one with more entries in the poll will have a higher chance to be selected. Try it out.

Dynamic AI

We can also use probability to specify the intelligence levels of AI characters, and the global game settings. This can in turn affect the overall difficulty level of the game, and keep it challenging and interesting enough to players. As described in the book, *The Art of Game Design, Jesse Schell, Morgan Kaufmann publications*, players will only continue to play our game if we keep them in their flow channel.

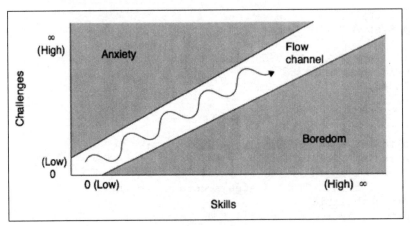

The Flow Channel

The players will feel anxious and get disappointed if we present tough challenges for them to solve before they have the necessary skills. On the other hand, once they've mastered the skills, and if we continue to keep the game at the same pace, then they will get bored. The grey area that can keep the players engaged for a long time is between these two extremes of hard and easy, which the original author referred to as the flow channel. To keep the players in the flow channel, the game designers need to feed the challenges and missions that match with the progressive skills that the players have acquired over time. However, it is not an easy task to find a value that works for all players, since the pace of learning and the expectations can be different individually.

One way to tackle this problem is to collect the player attempts and results during the game-play sessions, and to adjust the probability of the opponent's AI accordingly. Though this approach is supposed to help the games to be more engaging, there are many other players who don't like this approach, since this method takes away the pride and satisfaction of finishing a hard game. After all, beating a very hard boss AI character despite all the challenges can be much more rewarding and satisfying than winning the game because the AI is dumb. They would feel much worse if they find out that the AI becomes dumb because they don't have enough skills to match. So we must be careful about when we want to apply this technique in our games.

Demo slot machine

In this final demo, we'll design and implement a slot machine game with 10 symbols and three reels. Just to make it simple we'll just use the numbers from zero to nine as our symbols. Many slot machines would use fruit shapes and other simple shapes, such as bells, stars, and letters. Some other slot machines usually use a specific theme based on popular movies or TV programs as a franchise. Since there are 10 symbols and three reels, that's a total of 1,000 (10^3) possible combinations.

Random slot machine

This random slot machine demo is similar to our previous dice example. This time we are going to generate three random numbers for three reels. The only payout will be when you get three of the same symbols on the payline. To make it simpler, we'll only have one line to play against in this demo. And if the player wins, the game will return 500 times the bet amount.

We'll set up our scene with four GUI text objects to represent the three reels, and the result message.

Our GUI text objects

This is how our new script looks, as shown in the following `SlotMachine.cs` file::

```csharp
using UnityEngine;
using System.Collections;

public class SlotMachine : MonoBehaviour {

    public float spinDuration = 2.0f;
    public int numberOfSym = 10;
    private GameObject betResult;

    private bool startSpin = false;
    private bool firstReelSpinned = false;
    private bool secondReelSpinned = false;
    private bool thirdReelSpinned = false;

    private string betAmount = "100";

    private int firstReelResult = 0;
    private int secondReelResult = 0;
    private int thirdReelResult = 0;

    private float elapsedTime = 0.0f;

      //Use this for initialization
    void Start () {
      betResult = gameObject;
      betResult.guiText.text = "";
    }
```

```
void OnGUI() {
  GUI.Label(new Rect(200, 40, 100, 20), "Your bet: ");
  betAmount = GUI.TextField(new Rect(280, 40, 50, 20),
    betAmount, 25);
    if (GUI.Button(new Rect(200, 300, 150, 40),
      "Pull Liver")) {
    Start();
      startSpin = true;
    }
  }

void checkBet() {
  if (firstReelResult == secondReelResult &&
    secondReelResult == thirdReelResult) {
      betResult.guiText.text = "YOU WIN!";
    }
  else {
    betResult.guiText.text = "YOU LOSE!";
  }
}


  //Update is called once per frame
  void FixedUpdate () {
    if (startSpin) {
      elapsedTime += Time.deltaTime;
      int randomSpinResult = Random.Range(0,
        numberOfSym);
      if (!firstReelSpinned) {
      GameObject.Find("firstReel").guiText.text =
        randomSpinResult.ToString();
      if (elapsedTime >= spinDuration) {
        firstReelResult = randomSpinResult;
        firstReelSpinned = true;
        elapsedTime = 0;
      }
    }
      else if (!secondReelSpinned) {
        GameObject.Find("secondReel").guiText.text =
          randomSpinResult.ToString();
      if (elapsedTime >= spinDuration) {
        secondReelResult = randomSpinResult;
        secondReelSpinned = true;
        elapsedTime = 0;
      }
```

```
          }
       else if (!thirdReelSpinned) {
         GameObject.Find("thirdReel").guiText.text =
           randomSpinResult.ToString();
       if (elapsedTime >= spinDuration) {
         thirdReelResult = randomSpinResult;
           startSpin = false;
           elapsedTime = 0;
           firstReelSpinned = false;
           secondReelSpinned = false;
         checkBet();
         }
       }
     }
   }
 }
```

Attach the script to our `betResult` `guiText` object, and then position the `guiText` element on the screen. We have a button called **Pull Lever** in the `OnGUI()` method that will set the `startSpin` flag to true when clicked. And in our `FixedUpdate()` method we generate a random value for each reel if the `startSpin` is true. Finally, once we've got the value for the third reel, then we reset the `startSpin` to false. While we are getting the random value for each reel, we also keep a track of how much time has elapsed, since the player pulled the lever. Usually in the real world slot machines, each reel would take three to five seconds before landing the result. Hence, we are also taking some time as specified in `spinDuration` before showing the final random value. If you play the scene and click on the **Pull Lever** button, you should see the final result as shown in the following screenshot:

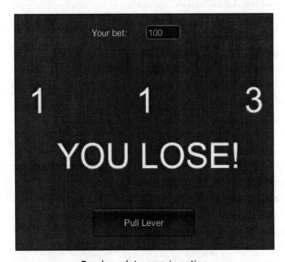

Random slot game in action

Since your chance of winning is one out of 100, it becomes boring as you lose several times consecutively. And of course if you've ever played a slot machine, this is not how it works, or at least not anymore. Usually you can have several wins during your play. Even though these small wins don't recoup your principal bet, and in the long run most of the players go broke, the slot machines would render winning graphics and winning sounds, which researchers referred to as losses disguised as wins.

So instead of just one single way to win—winning the jackpot—we'd like to modify the rules a bit so that it pays out smaller returns during the play session.

Weighted probability

Real slot machines have something called a **Paytable and Reel Strips (PARS)** sheet, which is like the complete design document of the machine. The PARS sheet is used to specify what the payout percentage is, what the winning patterns, and what their prizes are, and so on. Obviously the number of the payout prizes and the frequencies of such wins need to be carefully selected, so that the house (slot machine) can collect the fraction of the bets over time, while making sure to return the rest to the players to make the machine attractive to play. This is known as payback percentage or **return to player (RTP)**. For example, a slot machine with a 90 percent RTP means that over time the machine will return an average of 90 percent of all the bets to the players.

In this demo, we'll not be focusing on choosing the optimal value for the house to yield specific wins over time nor maintaining a particular payback percentage, but rather to demonstrate weighting probability to specific symbols, so that they show up more times than usual. So let's say we'd like to make the symbol zero to appear 20 percent more than by chance on the first and third reel, and return a small payout of half of the bet. In other words, a player will only lose half of their bet if they got zero symbols on the first and third reels, essentially disguising a loss as a small win. Currently, the zero symbol has a probability of $1/10$ (0.1) or 10 percent probability to occur. Now we'll make it 30 percent for zero to land on the first and third reels as shown in the following `SlotMachineWeighted.cs` file:

```
using UnityEngine;
using System.Collections;

public class SlotMachineWeighted : MonoBehaviour {
    public float spinDuration = 2.0f;
    public int numberOfSym = 10;
    public GameObject betResult;

    private bool startSpin = false;
    private bool firstReelSpinned = false;
```

```
private bool secondReelSpinned = false;
private bool thirdReelSpinned = false;

private int betAmount = 100;

private int creditBalance = 1000;
private ArrayList weightedReelPoll = new ArrayList();
private int zeroProbability = 30;

private int firstReelResult = 0;
private int secondReelResult = 0;
private int thirdReelResult = 0;

private float elapsedTime = 0.0f;
```

New variable declarations are added, such as zeroProbability to specify the probability percentage of the zero symbol to land on the first and third reels. The weightedReelPoll array list will be used to fill with all the symbols (zero to nine) according to their distribution, so that we can later pick one randomly from the poll like we did in our earlier FSM example. And then we initialize the list in our Start() method as shown in the following code:

```
void Start () {
  betResult = gameObject;
  betResult.guiText.text = "";
    for (int i = 0; i < zeroProbability; i++) {
      weightedReelPoll.Add(0);
    }
  nt remainingValuesProb = (100 - zeroProbability)/9;
    for (int j = 1; j < 10; j++) {
      for (int k = 0; k < remainingValuesProb; k++) {
        weightedReelPoll.Add(j);
      }
    }
}

void OnGUI() {
  GUI.Label(new Rect(150, 40, 100, 20), "Your bet: ");
  betAmount = int.Parse(GUI.TextField(new Rect(220, 40,
    50, 20), betAmount.ToString(), 25));
  GUI.Label(new Rect(300, 40, 100, 20), "Credits: " +
    creditBalance.ToString());
    if (GUI.Button(new Rect(200,300,150,40),"Pull Lever")) {
      betResult.guiText.text = "";
      startSpin = true;
    }
}
```

And the following is our revised `checkBet()` method. Instead of just one jackpot win, we are now considering five conditions: jackpot, loss disguised as win, near miss, any two symbols matched on the first and third row, and of course the lose condition:

```
void checkBet() {
  if (firstReelResult == secondReelResult &&
    secondReelResult == thirdReelResult) {
    betResult.guiText.text = "JACKPOT!";
    creditBalance += betAmount * 50;
    }
  else if (firstReelResult ==0 && thirdReelResult ==0) {
    betResult.guiText.text = "YOU WIN" +
      (betAmount/2).ToString();
      creditBalance -= (betAmount/2);
    }
  else if (firstReelResult == secondReelResult) {
    betResult.guiText.text = "AWW... ALMOST JACKPOT!";
    }
  else if (firstReelResult == thirdReelResult) {
    betResult.guiText.text = "YOU WIN" +
      (betAmount*2).ToString();
      creditBalance -= (betAmount*2);
    }
  else {
    betResult.guiText.text = "YOU LOSE!";
      creditBalance -= betAmount;
    }
  }
```

In the `checkBet()` method, we designed our slot machine to return 50 times if they hit the jackpot, only to lose 50 percent of their bet, if the first and third reels are zero, and two times if the first and third reels are matched with any other symbol. And we generate values for the three reels in the `FixedUpdate()` method as shown in the following code:

```
void FixedUpdate () {
  if (!startSpin) {
    return;
  }
    elapsedTime += Time.deltaTime;
    int randomSpinResult = Random.Range(0,
      numberOfSym);
    if (!firstReelSpinned) {
      GameObject.Find("firstReel").guiText.text =
        randomSpinResult.ToString();
    if (elapsedTime >= spinDuration) {
      int weightedRandom = Random.Range(0,
        weightedReelPoll.Count);
        GameObject.Find("firstReel").guiText.text =
```

```
            weightedReelPoll[weightedRandom].ToString();
            firstReelResult =
              (int)weightedReelPoll[weightedRandom];
            firstReelSpinned = true;
            elapsedTime = 0;
          }
        }
      else if (!secondReelSpinned) {
        GameObject.Find("secondReel").guiText.text =
          randomSpinResult.ToString();
      if (elapsedTime >= spinDuration) {
        secondReelResult = randomSpinResult;
        secondReelSpinned = true;
        elapsedTime = 0;
      }
    }
  }
```

For the first reel, during the spinning period, we really show the real random values. But once the time is up, we choose the value from our poll that is already populated with symbols according to the probability distributions. So our zero symbol would have 30 percent more chance of occurring than the rest, as shown in the following screenshot:

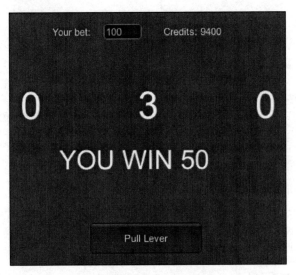

Loss disguised as a win

Actually the player is losing on his bets, if you get two zero symbols on the first and third reel. But we make it seem like a win. It's just a lame message here, but if we can combine it with nice graphics; maybe with fireworks, and nice winning sound effects, this can really work, and attract players to bet more, and pull that lever again and again.

Near miss

If the first and second reels return the same symbol, then we have to provide the near miss effect to the players by returning the random value to the third reel close to the second one. We can do this by checking the third random spin result first. If the random value is the same as the first and second results, then this is a jackpot, and we shouldn't alter the result. But if it's not, then we should modify the result so that it is close enough to the other two. Check the comments in the following code:

```
else if (!thirdReelSpinned) {
  GameObject.Find("thirdReel").guiText.text =
    randomSpinResult.ToString();
if (elapsedTime < spinDuration) {
  return;
}
if ((firstReelResult == secondReelResult)
  && randomSpinResult != firstReelResult) {
  randomSpinResult = firstReelResult - 1;
if (randomSpinResult < firstReelResult)
  randomSpinResult = firstReelResult - 1;
if (randomSpinResult > firstReelResult)
  randomSpinResult = firstReelResult + 1;
if (randomSpinResult < 0) randomSpinResult = 9;
if (randomSpinResult > 9) randomSpinResult = 0;
  GameObject.Find("thirdReel").guiText.text =
    randomSpinResult.ToString();
  thirdReelResult = randomSpinResult;
}
else {
  int weightedRandom = Random.Range(0,
    weightedReelPoll.Count);
  GameObject.Find("thirdReel").guiText.text =
    weightedReelPoll[weightedRandom].ToString();
  thirdReelResult =
    (int)weightedReelPoll[weightedRandom];
  }
  startSpin = false;
  elapsedTime = 0;
  firstReelSpinned = false;
  secondReelSpinned = false;
  checkBet();
}
}
}
```

And if that "near miss" happens, you should see it as shown in the following screenshot:

A near miss

We can go even further by adjusting the probability in real-time based on the bet amount. But that'd be too creepy. Another thing we could add to our game is a check to make sure the player can't bet more money than they already have. Also, we could add a game over message that appears when the player has bet all their money.

Summary

In this chapter, we learned about the applications of probability in the game AI design. We experimented with some of the techniques by implementing them in Unity3D. As a bonus, we also learnt about the basics of how a slot machine works, and implemented a simple slot machine game using Unity3D. Probability in game AI is about making the game and characters seem more realistic by adding some uncertainty, so that the players cannot predict something for sure. One of the common usages and definitions of probability is to measure the possibility of a desired event to occur out of all the other possible events. A good reference to further study the advanced techniques on probability in game AI, such as decision making under uncertainty using Bayesian techniques, would be the *AI for Game Developers David M. Bourg, Glenn Seeman, O'Reilly*. In the next chapter, we will take a look at implementing sensors, and how they can be used to make our AI aware of its surroundings.

4
Implementing Sensors

This is another short chapter on how to implement AI behaviors using the concept of a sensory system similar to what living entities have. As we have discussed earlier, a character AI system needs to have awareness of its environment, awareness such as where the obstacles are, where the enemy it's looking for is, if the enemy is visible in the player's sight, and others. The quality of artificial intelligence of our NPCs completely depends on the information it can get from the environment. Based on that information, the AI characters will decide which logic to execute. If there's not enough information for the AI, our AI characters can show strange behaviors, such as choosing the wrong places to take cover, idling, and looping strange actions, and not knowing what decision to make. Search for "AI glitches" on YouTube, and you'll find some funny behaviors of AI characters even in AAA games.

We can detect all the environment parameters and check against our predetermined values if we want. But using a proper design pattern will help us maintain code and thus will be easy to extend. This chapter will introduce such a design pattern that we can use to implement sensory systems. We will be going over what a sensory system is, and how to make such a system in Unity. We will then build a demo where we can see our sensory system in action.

Basic sensory systems

The AI sensory systems emulate senses such as perspectives, sounds, and even scents to track and identify objects. In game AI sensory systems, the agents will have to examine the environment and check for such senses periodically based on their particular interest.

The concept of a basic sensory system is that there will be two components: `Aspect` and `Sense`. Our AI characters will have senses, such as perception, smell, and touch. These senses will look out for specific aspects such as enemy and bandit. For example, you could have a patrol guard AI with a perception sense that's looking for other game objects with an enemy aspect. Or it could be a zombie entity with a smell sense looking for other entities with an aspect defined as brain.

For our demo, this is basically what we are going to implement: a base interface called `Sense` that will be implemented by other custom senses. In this chapter, we'll implement perspective and touch senses. Perspective is what animals use to see the world around them. If our AI character sees an enemy, we want to be notified so that we can take some action. Likewise, with Touch, when an enemy gets too close, we want to be able to sense that; almost as if our AI character can hear that the enemy is nearby. Then we'll write a minimal `Aspect` class that our senses will be looking for.

 RAIN{ONE} is an AI plugin for Unity3D that supports such a sensory system with not much coding required.

The following quote on RAIN has been taken from `http://rivaltheory.com/product`:

> *RAIN raises the bar for AI in Unity by giving in-game characters the ability to sense the world, pathfind, execute sophisticated behavior trees, and modify actions based on personality traits. All of this can even be accomplished with little to no coding experience.*

Scene setup

Let's get started setting up our scene. First let's create a few walls to block the line-of-sight from our AI character to the enemy. These will be short but wide cubes grouped under an empty game object called `Obstacles`. Next, we add a plane to be used as a floor. Then, we add a directional light, so we can see what is going on in our scene.

We will be going over this next part in detail throughout the chapter, but basically we will use a simple tank model for our player, and a simple cube for our AI character. We will also have a `Target` object to show us where the tank will move to in our scene. Our scene hierarchy will look similar to the following screenshot:

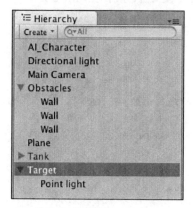

How our hiearchy is set up

Now we will position the tank, AI character, and walls randomly around in our scene. Increase the size of the plane to something that looks good. Fortunately, in this demo, our objects float, so nothing will fall off the plane. Also be sure to adjust the camera so that we can have a clear view of the following scene:

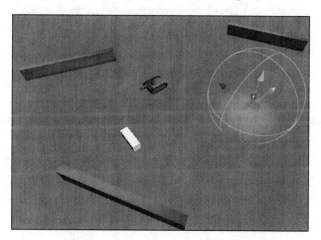

Where our tank and player will wander in

Now that we have the basics set up, we'll look at how to implement the tank, AI character, and aspects for our player character.

Player tank and aspect

Our `Target` object is a simple sphere object with the mesh render disabled. We have also created a point light and made it a child of our `Target` object. Make sure the light is centered, or it will not be very helpful for us.

Look at the following code in the `Target.cs` file:

```
using UnityEngine;
using System.Collections;

public class Target : MonoBehaviour {

  public Transform targetMarker;

  void Update () {
    int button = 0;
    //Get the point of the hit position when the mouse is being
 // clicked.
    if (Input.GetMouseButtonDown(button)) {
      Ray ray = Camera.main.ScreenPointToRay(Input.mousePosition);
      RaycastHit hitInfo;
      if (Physics.Raycast(ray.origin, ray.direction, out hitInfo)) {
        Vector3 targetPosition = hitInfo.point;
        targetMarker.position = targetPosition;
      }
    }
  }
}
```

Attach this script to our `Target` object. The script detects the mouse click event and then, using the raycasting technique, detects the mouse click point on the plane in the 3D space. After that it updates the `Target` object to that position in our scene.

Player tank

Our player tank is the simple tank model we used in the previous chapter with a non-kinematic rigid body component attached. The rigid body component is needed in order to generate trigger events whenever we do collision detection with any AI characters. The first thing we need to do is to assign the tag Player to our tank.

The tank is controlled by PlayerTank script, which we will create in a moment. This script retrieves the target position on the map, and updates its destination point and the direction accordingly.

The code in the PlayerTank.cs file is shown as follows:

```
using UnityEngine;
using System.Collections;

public class PlayerTank : MonoBehaviour {
  public Transform targetTransform;
  private float movementSpeed, rotSpeed;

  void Start () {
    movementSpeed = 10.0f;
    rotSpeed = 2.0f;
  }

  void Update () {
    //Stop once you reached near the target position
    if (Vector3.Distance(transform.position,
      targetTransform.position) < 5.0f)
      return;

    //Calculate direction vector from current position to target
//position
    Vector3 tarPos = targetTransform.position;
    tarPos.y = transform.position.y;
    Vector3 dirRot = tarPos - transform.position;

    //Build a Quaternion for this new rotation vector
    //using LookRotation method
    Quaternion tarRot = Quaternion.LookRotation(dirRot);
```

```
//Move and rotate with interpolation
transform.rotation= Quaternion.Slerp(transform.rotation,
    tarRot, rotSpeed * Time.deltaTime);

transform.Translate(new Vector3(0, 0,
    movementSpeed * Time.deltaTime));
    }
}
```

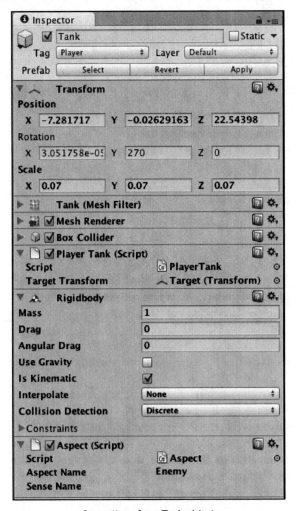

Properties of our Tank object

This script retrieves the position of the Target object on the map, and updates its destination point and the direction accordingly. After we assign this script to our tank, be sure to assign our Target object to the targetTransform variable.

Aspect

Next, let's take a look at the `Aspect.cs` class. `Aspect` is a very simple class with just one public property called `aspectName`. That's all the variables we need in this chapter. Whenever our AI character senses something, we'll check against with this `aspectName` if it's the aspect that the AI has been looking for.

The code in the `Aspect.cs` file is shown as follows:

```
using UnityEngine;
using System.Collections;

public class Aspect : MonoBehaviour {
  public enum aspect {
    Player,
    Enemy
  }
  public aspect aspectName;
}
```

Attach this aspect script to our player tank, and set the `aspectName` property as `Enemy`.

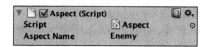

Setting which aspect to look out for

AI character

Our AI character will be roaming around the scene in a random direction. It'll have two senses: perspective and touch. The perspective sense will check whether the enemy aspect is within a set visible range and distance. Touch sense will detect if the enemy aspect has collided with the box collider, soon to be surrounding our AI character. As we have seen previously, our player tank will have `Enemy` aspect. So, these senses will be triggered when they detect the player tank.

The code in the `Wander.cs` file can be shown as follows:

```
using UnityEngine;
using System.Collections;

public class Wander : MonoBehaviour {
  private Vector3 tarPos;
```

```
private float movementSpeed = 5.0f;
private float rotSpeed = 2.0f;
private float minX, maxX, minZ, maxZ;

// Use this for initialization
void Start () {
  minX = -45.0f;
  maxX = 45.0f;

  minZ = -45.0f;
  maxZ = 45.0f;

  //Get Wander Position
  GetNextPosition();
}

// Update is called once per frame
void Update () {
  // Check if we're near the destination position
  if (Vector3.Distance(tarPos, transform.position) <= 5.0f)
    GetNextPosition(); //generate new random position

  // Set up quaternion for rotation toward destination
  Quaternion tarRot = Quaternion.LookRotation(tarPos -
      transform.position);

  // Update rotation and translation
  transform.rotation = Quaternion.Slerp(transform.rotation, tarRot,
      rotSpeed * Time.deltaTime);

  transform.Translate(new Vector3(0, 0,
      movementSpeed * Time.deltaTime));
}

void GetNextPosition() {
  tarPos = new Vector3(Random.Range(minX, maxX), 0.5f,
      Random.Range(minZ, maxZ));
}
}
```

The Wander script generates a new random position in a specified range whenever the AI character reaches its current destination point. The Update method will then rotate our enemy, and move it towards this new destination. Attach this script to our AI character so that it can move around in the scene.

Sense

The Sense class is the interface of our sensory system that the other custom senses can implement. It defines two virtual methods, Initialize and UpdateSense, which will be implemented in custom senses, and are executed from the Start and Update methods, respectively.

The code in the Sense.cs file can be shown as follows:

```
using UnityEngine;
using System.Collections;

public class Sense : MonoBehaviour {
  public bool bDebug = true;
  public Aspect.aspect aspectName = Aspect.aspect.Enemy;
  public float detectionRate = 1.0f;

  protected float elapsedTime = 0.0f;

  protected virtual void Initialize() { }
  protected virtual void UpdateSense() { }

  // Use this for initialization
  void Start () {
    elapsedTime = 0.0f;
    Initialize();
  }

  // Update is called once per frame
  void Update () {
    UpdateSense();
  }
}
```

Basic properties include its detection rate to execute the sensing operation as well as the name of the aspect it should look for. This script will not be attached to any of our objects.

Perspective

The perspective sense will detect whether a specific aspect is within its field of view and visible distance. If it sees anything, it will take the specified action.

The code in the Perspective.cs file can be shown as follows:

```
using UnityEngine;
using System.Collections;
```

```
public class Perspective : Sense {
  public int FieldOfView = 45;
  public int ViewDistance = 100;

  private Transform playerTrans;
  private Vector3 rayDirection;

  protected override void Initialize() {

    //Find player position
    playerTrans =

GameObject.FindGameObjectWithTag("Player").transform;
  }

  // Update is called once per frame
  protected override void UpdateSense() {
    elapsedTime += Time.deltaTime;

    // Detect perspective sense if within the detection rate
    if (elapsedTime >= detectionRate) DetectAspect();
  }

  //Detect perspective field of view for the AI Character
  void DetectAspect() {
    RaycastHit hit;

    //Direction from current position to player position
    rayDirection = playerTrans.position -
        transform.position;

    //Check the angle between the AI character's forward
    //vector and the direction vector between player and AI
    if ((Vector3.Angle(rayDirection, transform.forward)) <
FieldOfView) {
      // Detect if player is within the field of view
      if (Physics.Raycast(transform.position, rayDirection,
        out hit, ViewDistance)) {
        Aspect aspect =
        hit.collider.GetComponent<Aspect>();

        if (aspect != null) {
          //Check the aspect
          if (aspect.aspectName == aspectName) {
            print("Enemy Detected");
          }
        }
      }
    }
  }
```

We need to implement `Initialize` and `UpdateSense` methods that will be called from the `Start` and `Update` methods of the parent `Sense` class, respectively. Then, in the `DetectAspect` method, we first check the angle between the player and the AI's current direction. If it's in the field of view range, we shoot a ray in the direction where the player tank is located. The ray length is the value of visible distance property. The `Raycast` method will return when it first hits another object. Then, we'll check against the aspect component and the aspect name. This way, even if the player is in the visible range, the AI character will not be able to see if it's hidden behind the wall.

The `OnDrawGizmos` method draws lines based on the perspective field of view angle and viewing distance, so that we can see the AI character's line-of-sight in the editor window during play testing. Attach this script to our AI character, and be sure that the aspect name is set to `Enemy`.

This method can be illustrated as follows:

```
void OnDrawGizmos() {
    if (!bDebug || playerTrans == null) return;

    Debug.DrawLine(transform.position, playerTrans.position, Color.
red);

    Vector3 frontRayPoint = transform.position +
        (transform.forward * ViewDistance);

    //Approximate perspective visualization
    Vector3 leftRayPoint = frontRayPoint;
    leftRayPoint.x += FieldOfView * 0.5f;

    Vector3 rightRayPoint = frontRayPoint;
    rightRayPoint.x -= FieldOfView * 0.5f;

    Debug.DrawLine(transform.position, frontRayPoint, Color.green);

    Debug.DrawLine(transform.position, leftRayPoint, Color.green);

    Debug.DrawLine(transform.position, rightRayPoint, Color.green);
    }
}
```

Touch

Another sense we're going to implement is `Touch.cs`, which is triggered when the player entity is within a certain area near the AI entity. Our AI character has a box collider component, and its `Is Trigger` flag is on.

We need to implement `OnTriggerEnter` event that will be fired whenever the collider component is collided with another collider component. Since our tank entity also has a collider and rigid body components, collision events will be raised as soon as the colliders of the AI character and player tank are collided.

The code in the `Touch.cs` file can be shown as follows:

```
using UnityEngine;
using System.Collections;

public class Touch : Sense {
  void OnTriggerEnter(Collider other) {
    Aspect aspect = other.GetComponent<Aspect>();
    if (aspect != null) {
      //Check the aspect
      if (aspect.aspectName == aspectName) {
        print("Enemy Touch Detected");
      }
    }
  }
}
```

We implement the `OnTriggerEnter` event to be fired whenever the collider component is collided with another collider component. Since our tank entity also has a collider and the rigid body components, collision events will be raised as soon as the colliders of the AI character and the player tank are collided.

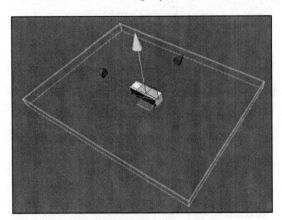

The collider around our player

The previous figure shows the box collider of our enemy AI that we'll use to implement touch sense. In the following screenshot, we see how our AI character is set up.

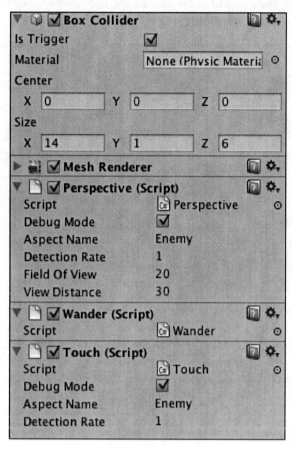

Properties of our player

Inside the `OnTriggerEnter` method, we access the aspect component of the other collided entity and check if the name of the aspect is the aspect this AI character is looking for. And, for demo purposes, we just print out that the enemy aspect has been detected by touch sense. We can also implement other behaviors if in real projects; maybe the player will turn over to an enemy and start chasing, attacking, and so on.

Testing

Play the game in Unity3D, and move the player tank near the wandering AI character by clicking the ground. You should see the **Enemy touch detected** message in the console log window whenever our AI character gets close to our player tank.

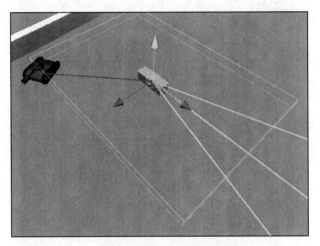

Our player and tank in action

The previous figure shows an AI agent with touch and perspective senses looking for an enemy aspect. Move the player tank in front of the AI character, and you'll get the **Enemy detected** message. If you go to the editor view while running the game, you should see the debug drawings rendered. This is because of the OnDrawGizmos method implemented in the perspective Sense class.

Summary

This chapter introduces the concept of using sensors in implementing game AI, and implemented two senses, perspective and touch, for our AI character. The sensory system is just part of the decision-making system of the whole AI system. We can use the sensory system in combination with a behavior system to execute certain behaviors for certain senses. For example, we can use an FSM to change to chase and attack states from the patrol state once we have detected that there's an enemy within the line-of-sight. We'll also cover how to apply behavior tree systems in *Chapter 9, Behavior Trees*. In the next chapter, we'll look at how to implement flocking behaviors in Unity3D, as well as how to implement Craig Reynold's flocking algorithm.

5
Flocking

Flocking is the idea of many objects moving together as a group. We could sit down and tell every object how it should move, but that would take a lot of work. Instead, we want to be able to create a flock leader to do that for us. After that, all we need is a few rules and the boids will be flocking all on their own. In this chapter, we'll learn how to do that and implement flocking behavior in Unity3D.

We'll implement two variations of flocking in this chapter. The first one will be based on a sample flocking behavior found in a demo project called Tropical Paradise Island. This demo came with Unity in Version 2.0, but has been removed since Unity 3.0. The second variation will be based on Craig Reynold's flocking algorithm. There are basically three rules that can be applied to each boid:

- **Separation**: To maintain a distance with other neighbors in the flock to avoid collision
- **Alignment**: To move in the same direction as the flock, and with the same velocity
- **Cohesion**: To maintain a minimum distance with the flock's center

Flocking from Unity's Island Demo

In this section, we'll create our own scene with flocks of objects and implement the flocking behavior in C#. There are two main components in this example: the individual boid behavior and a main controller to maintain and lead the crowd.

Our scene hierarchy is shown in the following screenshot. As you can see, we have several boid entities, **UnityFlock,** under a controller named **UnityFlockController.** **UnityFlock** entities are individual boid objects, and they'll reference to their parent **UnityFlockController** entity to use it as a leader. **UnityFlockController** will update the next destination point randomly once it reaches the current destination point.

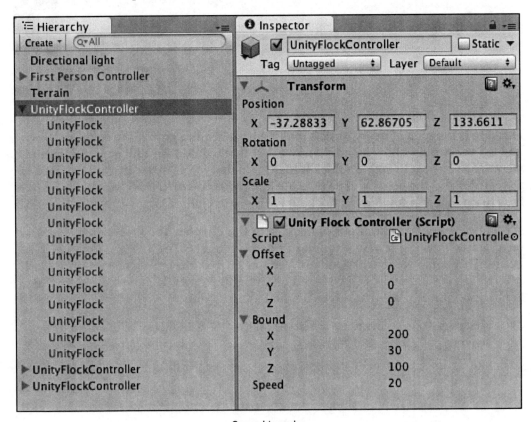

Scene hierarchy

UnityFlock is a prefab with just a cube mesh and a **UnityFlock** script. We can use any other mesh representation for this prefab to represent something more interesting like birds.

Individual Behavior

Boid is a term coined by Craig Reynold that refers to some bird like object. We'll use this term to describe each individual object in our flock. Now let's implement our boid behavior. You can find the following script in UnityFlock.cs, and this is the behavior that controls each boid in our flock.

The code in the `UnityFlock.cs` file can be shown as follows:

```
using UnityEngine;
using System.Collections;

public class UnityFlock : MonoBehaviour {
    public float minSpeed = 20.0f;
    public float turnSpeed = 20.0f;
    public float randomFreq = 20.0f;
    public float randomForce = 20.0f;

    //alignment variables
    public float toOriginForce = 50.0f;
    public float toOriginRange = 100.0f;

    public float gravity = 2.0f;

    //seperation variables
    public float avoidanceRadius = 50.0f;
    public float avoidanceForce = 20.0f;

    //cohesion variables
    public float followVelocity = 4.0f;
    public float followRadius = 40.0f;

    //these variables control the movement of the boid
    private Transform origin;
    private Vector3 velocity;
    private Vector3 normalizedVelocity;
    private Vector3 randomPush;
    private Vector3 originPush;
    private Transform[] objects;
    private UnityFlock[] otherFlocks;
    private Transform transformComponent;
```

We declare the input values for our algorithm that can be set up and customized from the editor. First, we define the minimum movement speed, `minSpeed` and rotation speed, `turnSpeed`, for our boid. `randomFreq` is used to determine how many times we want to update the `randomPush` value based on the `randomForce` value. This force creates a randomly increased and decreased velocity and makes the flock movement look more realistic.

`toOriginRange` specifies how spread out we want our flock to be. We also use `toOriginForce` to keep the boids in range and maintain a distance with the flock's origin. Basically, these are the properties to deal with the alignment rule of our flocking algorithm. The `avoidanceRadius` and `avoidanceForce` properties are used to maintain a minimum distance between individual boids. These are the properties that apply the separation rule to our flock.

`followRadius` and `followVelocity` are used to keep a minimum distance with the leader or the origin of the flock. They are used to comply with the cohesion rule of the flocking algorithm.

`origin` will be the parent object to control the whole group of flocking objects. Our boid needs to know about the other boids in the flock. So, we use the `objects` and `otherFlocks` properties to store the neighboring boids' information.

This is the initialization method for our boid:

```
void Start () {
  randomFreq = 1.0f / randomFreq;

  //Assign the parent as origin
  origin = transform.parent;

  //Flock transform
  transformComponent = transform;

  //Temporary components
  Component[] tempFlocks= null;

  //Get all the unity flock components from the parent
  //transform in the group
  if (transform.parent) {
    tempFlocks = transform.parent.GetComponentsInChildren
        <UnityFlock>();
  }

  //Assign and store all the flock objects in this group
  objects = new Transform[tempFlocks.Length];
  otherFlocks = new UnityFlock[tempFlocks.Length];

  for (int i = 0;i<tempFlocks.Length;i++) {
    objects[i] = tempFlocks[i].transform;
    otherFlocks[i] = (UnityFlock)tempFlocks[i];
  }
```

```
    //Null Parent as the flock leader will be
    //UnityFlockController object
    transform.parent = null;

    //Calculate random push depends on the random frequency
//provided
    StartCoroutine(UpdateRandom());
  }
```

We set the parent of the object of our boid as `origin`, meaning that this will be the controller object to follow generally. Then, we grab all the other boids in the group and store them in our own variables for later references.

The `StartCoroutine` method starts the `UpdateRandom()` method as a coroutine:

```
IEnumerator UpdateRandom() {
  while (true) {
    randomPush = Random.insideUnitSphere * randomForce;
    yield return new WaitForSeconds(randomFreq +
        Random.Range(-randomFreq / 2.0f, randomFreq / 2.0f));
  }
}
```

The `UpdateRandom()` method updates the `randomPush` value throughout the game with an interval based on `randomFreq`. `Random.insideUnitSphere` returns a `Vector3` object with random *x*, *y*, and *z* values within a sphere with a radius of the `randomForce` value. Then, we wait for a certain random amount of time before resuming the `while(true)` loop to update the `randomPush` value again.

Now, here's our boid behavior's `Update()` method that helps our boid entity comply with the three rules of the flocking algorithm:

```
void Update () {
  //Internal variables
  float speed = velocity.magnitude;
  Vector3 avgVelocity = Vector3.zero;
  Vector3 avgPosition = Vector3.zero;
  float count = 0;
  float f = 0.0f;
  float d = 0.0f;
  Vector3 myPosition = transformComponent.position;
  Vector3 forceV;
  Vector3 toAvg;
  Vector3 wantedVel;
```

```
for (int i = 0;i<objects.Length;i++){
  Transform transform= objects[i];
  if (transform != transformComponent) {
    Vector3 otherPosition = transform.position;

    // Average position to calculate cohesion
    avgPosition += otherPosition;
    count++;

    //Directional vector from other flock to this flock
    forceV = myPosition - otherPosition;

    //Magnitude of that directional vector(Length)
    d= forceV.magnitude;

    //Add push value if the magnitude, the length of the
    //vector, is less than followRadius to the leader
    if (d < followRadius) {
      //calculate the velocity, the speed of the object, based
       //on the avoidance distance between flocks if the
      //current magnitude is less than the specified
      //avoidance radius
      if (d < avoidanceRadius) {
        f = 1.0f - (d / avoidanceRadius);
        if (d > 0) avgVelocity +=
            (forceV / d) * f * avoidanceForce;
      }

      //just keep the current distance with the leader
      f = d / followRadius;
      UnityFlock otherSealgull = otherFlocks[i];
      //we normalize the otherSealgull velocity vector to get
      //the direction of movement, then we set a new velocity
      avgVelocity += otherSealgull.normalizedVelocity * f *
          followVelocity;
    }
  }
}
```

The preceding code implements the separation rule. First, we check the distance between the current boid and the other boids and update the velocity accordingly, as explained in the comments.

Next, we calculate the average velocity of the flock by dividing the current velocity with the number of boids in the flock:

```
if (count > 0) {
  //Calculate the average flock velocity(Alignment)
  avgVelocity /= count;
```

```
      //Calculate Center value of the flock(Cohesion)
      toAvg = (avgPosition / count) - myPosition;
   }
   else {
      toAvg = Vector3.zero;
   }

   //Directional Vector to the leader
   forceV = origin.position -  myPosition;
   d = forceV.magnitude;
   f = d / toOriginRange;

   //Calculate the velocity of the flock to the leader
   if (d > 0) //if this void is not at the center of the flock
       originPush = (forceV / d) * f * toOriginForce;

   if (speed < minSpeed && speed > 0) {
      velocity = (velocity / speed) * minSpeed;
   }

   wantedVel = velocity;

   //Calculate final velocity
   wantedVel -= wantedVel *  Time.deltaTime;
   wantedVel += randomPush * Time.deltaTime;
   wantedVel += originPush * Time.deltaTime;
   wantedVel += avgVelocity * Time.deltaTime;
   wantedVel += toAvg.normalized * gravity * Time.deltaTime;

   //Final Velocity to rotate the flock into
   velocity = Vector3.RotateTowards(velocity, wantedVel,
       turnSpeed * Time.deltaTime, 100.00f);

   transformComponent.rotation =
Quaternion.LookRotation(velocity);

   //Move the flock based on the calculated velocity
   transformComponent.Translate(velocity * Time.deltaTime,
       Space.World);

   //normalise the velocity
   normalizedVelocity = velocity.normalized;
  }
}
```

Finally, we add up all the factors such as `randomPush`, `originPush`, and `avgVelocity` to calculate our final target velocity, `wantedVel`. We also update our current `velocity` to `wantedVel` with linear interpolation using the `Vector3.RotateTowards` method. Then, we move our boid based on the new velocity using the `Translate()` method.

Next, we create a cube mesh, and add this **UnityFlock** script, and make it a prefab as shown in the following screenshot:

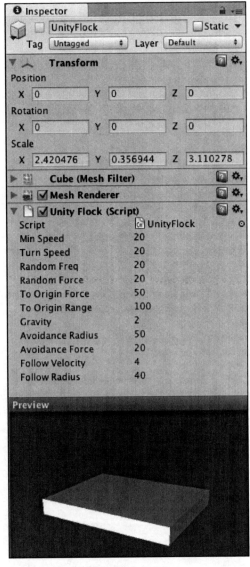

Unity flock prefab

Controller

Now it is time to create the controller class. This class updates its own position so that the other individual boid objects know where to go. This object is referenced in the `origin` variable in the preceding **UnityFlock** script.

The code in the `UnityFlockController.cs` file can be shown as follows:

```
using UnityEngine;
using System.Collections;

public class UnityFlockController : MonoBehaviour {
  public Vector3 offset;
  public Vector3 bound;
  public float speed = 100.0f;

  private Vector3 initialPosition;
  private Vector3 nextMovementPoint;

  // Use this for initialization
  void Start () {
    initialPosition = transform.position;
    CalculateNextMovementPoint();
  }

  // Update is called once per frame
  void Update () {
    transform.Translate(Vector3.forward * speed * Time.deltaTime);
    transform.rotation = Quaternion.Slerp(transform.rotation,
        Quaternion.LookRotation(nextMovementPoint -
        transform.position), 1.0f * Time.deltaTime);

    if (Vector3.Distance(nextMovementPoint,
        transform.position) <= 10.0f)
        CalculateNextMovementPoint();
  }
```

In our `Update()` method, we check whether our controller object is near the target destination point. If it is, we update our `nextMovementPoint` variable again with the `CalculateNextMovementPoint()` method we just discussed:

```
  void CalculateNextMovementPoint () {
    float posX = Random.Range(initialPosition.x - bound.x,
        initialPosition.x + bound.x);
    float posY = Random.Range(initialPosition.y - bound.y,
```

```
        initialPosition.y + bound.y);
    float posZ = Random.Range(initialPosition.z - bound.z,
        initialPosition.z + bound.z);

    nextMovementPoint = initialPosition + new Vector3(posX,
        posY, posZ);
    }
}
```

The `CalculateNextMovementPoint()` method finds the next random destination position in a range between the current position and the boundary vectors.

Putting it all together, as shown in the previous scene hierarchy screenshot, you should have flocks flying around somewhat realistically:

Flocking using the Unity seagull sample

Alternative implementation

Here's a simpler implementation of the flocking algorithm. In this example, we'll create a cube object and place a rigid body on our boids. With Unity's rigid body physics, we can simplify the translation and steering behavior of our boid. To prevent our boids from overlapping each other, we'll add a sphere collider physics component.

We'll have two components in this implementation as well: individual boid behavior and controller behavior. The controller will be the object that the rest of the boids try and follow.

The code in the `Flock.cs` file can be shown as follows:

```
using UnityEngine;
using System.Collections;
using System.Collections.Generic;

public class Flock : MonoBehaviour {
  internal FlockController controller;

  void Update () {
    if (controller) {
      Vector3 relativePos = steer() * Time.deltaTime;

      if (relativePos != Vector3.zero)
          rigidbody.velocity = relativePos;

      // enforce minimum and maximum speeds for the boids
      float speed = rigidbody.velocity.magnitude;
      if (speed > controller.maxVelocity) {
        rigidbody.velocity = rigidbody.velocity.normalized *
          controller.maxVelocity;
      }
      else if (speed < controller.minVelocity) {
        rigidbody.velocity = rigidbody.velocity.normalized *
            controller.minVelocity;
      }
    }
  }
}
```

FlockController will be created in a moment. In our Update() method, we calculate the velocity for our boid using the following steer() method and apply it to its rigid body velocity. Next, we check the current speed of our rigid body component to verify whether it's in the range of our controller's maximum and minimum velocity limits. If not, we cap the velocity at the preset range:

```
private Vector3 steer () {
  Vector3 center = controller.flockCenter -
      transform.localPosition;  // cohesion

  Vector3 velocity = controller.flockVelocity -
      rigidbody.velocity;  // alignment

  Vector3 follow = controller.target.localPosition -
      transform.localPosition;  // follow leader

  Vector3 separation = Vector3.zero;

  foreach (Flock flock in controller.flockList) {
    if (flock != this) {
      Vector3 relativePos = transform.localPosition -
          flock.transform.localPosition;

      separation += relativePos / (relativePos.sqrMagnitude);
    }
  }

  // randomize
  Vector3 randomize = new Vector3( (Random.value * 2) - 1,
      (Random.value * 2) - 1, (Random.value * 2) - 1);

  randomize.Normalize();

  return (controller.centerWeight * center +
      controller.velocityWeight * velocity +
      controller.separationWeight * separation +
      controller.followWeight * follow +
      controller.randomizeWeight * randomize);
  }
}
```

The `steer()` method implements separation, cohesion, alignment, and follows the leader rules of the flocking algorithm. Then, we sum up all the factors together with a random weight value. With this **Flock** script together with rigid body and sphere collider components, we create a **Flock** prefab as shown in the following screenshot:

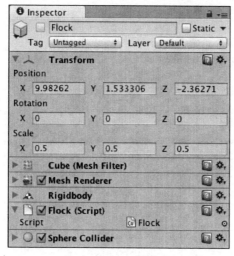

Flock

FlockController

FlockController is a simple behavior to generate the boids at runtime and update the center of the flock as well as the average velocity of the flock.

The code in the `FlockController.cs` file can be shown as follows:

```
using UnityEngine;
using System.Collections;
using System.Collections.Generic;

public class FlockController : MonoBehaviour {
  public float minVelocity = 1;  //Min Velocity
  public float maxVelocity = 8;  //Max Flock speed
  public int flockSize = 20;  //Number of flocks in the group

  //How far the boids should stick to the center (the more
  //weight stick closer to the center)
  public float centerWeight = 1;

  public float velocityWeight = 1;  //Alignment behavior
```

```
//How far each boid should be separated within the flock
public float separationWeight = 1;

//How close each boid should follow to the leader (the more
//weight make the closer follow)
public float followWeight = 1;

//Additional Random Noise
public float randomizeWeight = 1;

public Flock prefab;
public Transform target;

//Center position of the flock in the group
internal Vector3 flockCenter;
internal Vector3 flockVelocity;   //Average Velocity

public ArrayList flockList = new ArrayList();

void Start () {
  for (int i = 0; i < flockSize; i++) {
    Flock flock = Instantiate(prefab, transform.position,
        transform.rotation) as Flock;
    flock.transform.parent = transform;
    flock.controller = this;
    flockList.Add(flock);
  }
}
```

We declare all the properties to implement the flocking algorithm and then start with the generation of the boid objects based on the flock size input. We set up the controller class and parent transform object like we did last time. Then, we add the created boid object in our `ArrayList` function. The `target` variable accepts an entity to be used as a moving leader. We'll create a sphere entity as a moving target leader for our flock:

```
void Update () {
  //Calculate the Center and Velocity of the whole flock group
  Vector3 center = Vector3.zero;
  Vector3 velocity = Vector3.zero;

  foreach (Flock flock in flockList) {
    center += flock.transform.localPosition;
    velocity += flock.rigidbody.velocity;
  }
```

```
        flockCenter = center / flockSize;
        flockVelocity = velocity / flockSize;
    }
}
```

In our `Update()` method, we keep updating the average center and velocity of the flock. Those are the values referenced from our boid object, and they are used to adjust the cohesion and alignment properties with the controller.

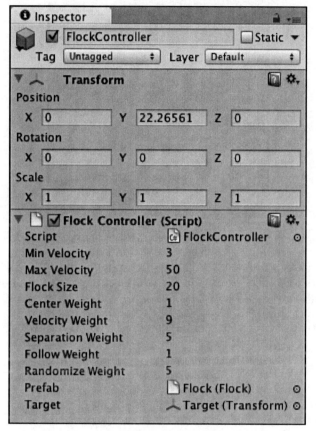

Flock controller

Following is our **Target** entity with the TargetMovement script, which we will create in a moment. The movement script is the same as we have seen in our previous Unity3D sample controller's movement script:

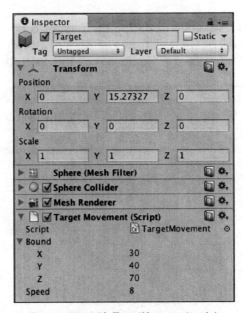

Target entity with TargetMovement script

Here is how our TargetMovement script works. We pick a random point nearby for the target to move to. When we get close to that point, pick a new point. The boids will then follow the target.

The code in the TargetMovement.cs file can be shown as follows:

```
using UnityEngine;
using System.Collections;

public class TargetMovement : MonoBehaviour {
  //Move target around circle with tangential speed
  public Vector3 bound;
  public float speed = 100.0f;

  private Vector3 initialPosition;
  private Vector3 nextMovementPoint;

  void Start () {
    initialPosition = transform.position;
    CalculateNextMovementPoint();
  }
```

```
void CalculateNextMovementPoint () {
  float posX = Random.Range(initialPosition.x = bound.x,
      initialPosition.x+bound.x);
  float posY = Random.Range(initialPosition.y = bound.y,
      initialPosition.y+bound.y);
  float posZ = Random.Range(initialPosition.z = bound.z,
      initialPosition.z+bound.z);

  nextMovementPoint = initialPosition+
      new Vector3(posX, posY, posZ);
}
void Update () {
  transform.Translate(Vector3.forward * speed * Time.deltaTime);
  transform.rotation = Quaternion.Slerp(transform.rotation,
      Quaternion.LookRotation(nextMovementPoint -
      transform.position), 1.0f * Time.deltaTime);

  if (Vector3.Distance(nextMovementPoint, transform.position)
      <= 10.0f) CalculateNextMovementPoint();
  }
}
```

After we put everything together, we should have nice flocking boids flying around in our scene chasing that target:

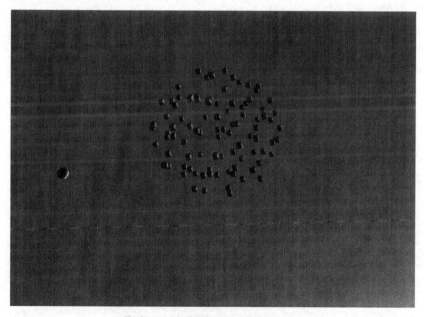

Flocking with Craig Reynold's algorithm

Summary

In this chapter, we learned how to implement flocking behavior in two ways. First we examined, dissected, and learned how to implement a flocking algorithm based on Unity3D's Tropical Island Demo project. Next, we implemented using rigid body to control the boid's movement and sphere collider to avoid collision with other boids. We applied our flocking behavior to the flying objects, but you can apply the techniques in those examples to implement other character behaviors such as fish shoaling, insects swarming, or land animals herding. You'll only have to implement different leader movement behaviors such as limiting movement along the y-axis for characters that can't move up and down. For a 2D game, we would just freeze the y position. For 2D movement along uneven terrain, we would have to modify our script to not put any forces in the y direction.

In the next chapter, we will go beyond random movement and take a look at path following. We will also be going over how to avoid obstacles that are in your way.

6
Path Following and Steering Behaviors

This will be a simple and short chapter, and we will implement two Unity3D scenes. In the first example, we'll set up a scene with a path and will write some script to make an entity follow this path. In the second example, we'll set up a scene with a couple of obstacles and program an entity to achieve a target while avoiding the obstacles. Obstacle avoidance is a simple behavior for the AI entities to reach a target point. It's important to note that the specific behavior implemented in this chapter is meant to use for behaviors, such as crowd simulation, where the main objective of each agent entity is just to avoid the other agents and reach the target. There's no consideration on what would be the most efficient and shortest path. We'll learn about the A* pathfinding algorithm in the next chapter.

Following a path

Paths are usually created by connecting waypoints together. So, we'll set up a simple path as shown in the following figure and then make our cube entity follow along the path smoothly. Now, there are many ways to build such a path. The one we are going to implement here could arguably be the simplest one. We'll write a script called `Path.cs` and store all the waypoint positions in a `Vector3` array. Then, from the editor, we'll enter those positions manually. It's bit of a tedious process right now. One option is to use the position of an empty game object as waypoints. Or, if you want, you can create your own editor plugins to automate these kind of tasks, but that is outside the scope of this book. For now, it should be fine to just enter the waypoint information manually, since the number of waypoints that we are creating here are not that substantial.

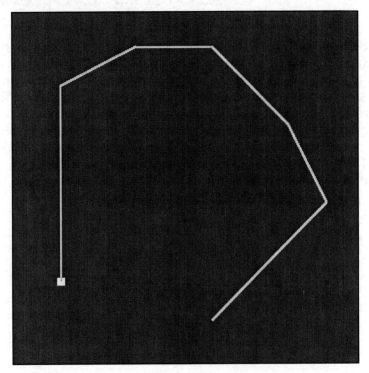

Object path

First, we create an empty game entity and add our path script component as shown in the following screenshot:

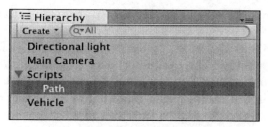

Here is how the Hierarchy is organized

Then, we populate our **Point A** variable with all the points we want to be included in our path:

Path (Script)		
Script	Path	
BDebug	✓	
Radius	2	
▼ Point A		
Size	8	
▼ Element 0		
X	0	
Y	0	
Z	0	
▼ Element 1		
X	0	
Y	0	
Z	25	
▼ Element 2		
X	10	
Y	0	
Z	30	
▼ Element 3		
X	20	
Y	0	
Z	30	
▼ Element 4		
X	25	
Y	0	
Z	25	
▼ Element 5		
X	30	
Y	0	
Z	20	
▼ Element 6		
X	35	
Y	0	
Z	10	
▼ Element 7		
X	20	
Y	0	
Z	-5	

Properties of our Path script

The previous list shows the waypoints needed to create the path that was described earlier. The other two properties are debug mode and radius. If the debug mode property is checked, the path formed by the positions entered will be drawn as gizmos in the editor window. The radius property is a range value for the path following entities to use so that they can know when they've reached a particular waypoint if they are in this radius range. Since to reach an exact position can be pretty difficult, this range radius value provides an effective way for the path following agents to navigate through the path.

Path script

So let's take a look at the path script itself. It will be responsible for managing the path for our objects. Look at the following code in the Path.cs file:

```
using UnityEngine;
using System.Collections;

public class Path : MonoBehaviour {
  public bool bDebug = true;
  public float Radius = 2.0f;
  public Vector3[] pointA;

  public float Length {
    get {
      return pointA.Length;
    }
  }

  public Vector3 GetPoint(int index) {
    return pointA[index];
  }

  void OnDrawGizmos() {
    if (!bDebug) return;

    for (int i = 0; i <pointA.Length; i++) {
      if (i + 1<pointA.Length) {
        Debug.DrawLine(pointA[i], pointA[i + 1],
          Color.red);
      }
    }
  }
}
```

As you can see, that is a very simple script. It has a `Length` property that returns the length and size of the waypoint array if requested. The `GetPoint` method returns the `Vector3` position of a particular waypoint at a specified index in the array. Then, we have the `OnDrawGizmos` method that is called by Unity3D frame to draw components in the editor environment. The drawing here won't be rendered in the game view unless gizmos, located in the top right corner of the game view, is turned on.

Path follower

Next we have our vehicle entity, which is just a simple cube object in this example. We can replace the cube later with whatever 3D models we want. After we create the script, we add the **VehicleFollowing** script component as shown in the following screenshot:

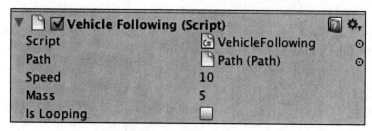

Properties of our Vehicle Following script

The script takes a couple of parameters. First is the reference to the path object it needs to follow. Then, the **Speed** and **Mass** properties, which are needed to calculate its acceleration properly. **Is Looping** is a flag that makes this entity follow the path continuously if it's checked. Let's take a look at the following code in the `VehicleFollowing.cs` file:

```
using UnityEngine;
using System.Collections;

public class VehicleFollowing : MonoBehaviour {
  public Path path;
  public float speed = 20.0f;
  public float mass = 5.0f;
  public bool isLooping = true;

  //Actual speed of the vehicle
  private float curSpeed;
```

```
private int curPathIndex;
private float pathLength;
private Vector3 targetPoint;

Vector3 velocity;
```

First, we initialize the properties and set up the direction of our velocity vector with the entity's forward vector in the `Start` method, as shown in the following code:

```
void Start () {
  pathLength = path.Length;
  curPathIndex = 0;

  //get the current velocity of the vehicle
  velocity = transform.forward;
}
```

There are only two methods that are important in this script, the `Update` and `Steer` methods. Let's take a look at the following code:

```
void Update () {
  //Unify the speed
  curSpeed = speed * Time.deltaTime;

  targetPoint = path.GetPoint(curPathIndex);

  //If reach the radius within the path then move to next
    //point in the path
      if (Vector3.Distance(transform.position, targetPoint) <
        path.Radius) {
        //Don't move the vehicle if path is finished
      if (curPathIndex < pathLength - 1) curPathIndex++;
        else if (isLooping) curPathIndex = 0;
        else return;
  }

  //Move the vehicle until the end point is reached in
    //the path
      if (curPathIndex >= pathLength ) return;

  //Calculate the next Velocity towards the path
      if (curPathIndex >= pathLength-1&& !isLooping)
        velocity += Steer(targetPoint, true);
        else velocity += Steer(targetPoint);
```

```
//Move the vehicle according to the velocity
  transform.position += velocity;
//Rotate the vehicle towards the desired Velocity
  transform.rotation = Quaternion.LookRotation(velocity);
}
```

In the Update method, we check whether our entity has reached a particular waypoint by calculating the distance between its current position and the path's radius range. If it's in the range, we just increase the index to look it up from the waypoints array. If it's the last waypoint, we check if the isLooping flag is set. If it is set, then we set the target to the starting waypoint. Otherwise, we just stop at that point. Though, if we wanted, we could make it so our object turned around and went back the way it came. In the next part, we will calculate the acceleration from the Steer method. Then, we rotate our entity and update the position according to the speed and direction of the velocity:

```
//Steering algorithm to steer the vector towards the target
  public Vector3 Steer(Vector3 target,
    bool bFinalPoint = false) {
  //Calculate the directional vector from the current
    //position towards the target point
  Vector3 desiredVelocity = (target -transform.position);
  float dist = desiredVelocity.magnitude;

  //Normalise the desired Velocity
  desiredVelocity.Normalize();

  //Calculate the velocity according to the speed
  if (bFinalPoint&&dist<10.0f) desiredVelocity *=
    (curSpeed * (dist / 10.0f));
    else desiredVelocity *= curSpeed;

  //Calculate the force Vector
  Vector3 steeringForce = desiredVelocity - velocity;
  Vector3 acceleration = steeringForce / mass;

  return acceleration;
  }
}
```

The `Steer` method takes the parameter; target `Vector3` position to move, whether this is the final waypoint in the path. The first thing we do is calculate the remaining distance from the current position to the target position. The target position vector minus the current position vector gives a vector towards the target position vector. The magnitude of this vector is the remaining distance. We then normalize this vector just to preserve the `direction` property. Now, if this is the final waypoint, and the distance is less than `10` of a number we just decided to use, we slow down the velocity gradually according to the remaining distance to our point until the velocity finally becomes zero. Otherwise, we just update the target velocity with the specified speed value. By subtracting the current velocity vector from this target velocity vector, we can calculate the new steering vector. Then by dividing this vector with the mass value of our entity, we get the acceleration.

If you run the scene, you should see your cube object following the path. You can also see the path that is drawn in the editor view. Play around with the speed and mass value of the follower and radius values of the path and see how they affect the overall behavior of the system.

Avoiding obstacles

In this section, we'll set up a scene as shown in the following screenshot, and make our AI entity avoid the obstacles while trying to reach the target point. The algorithm presented here using the `raycasting` method is very simple, so it can only avoid the obstacles blocking the path in front of it. The following screenshot will show us what our scene will look like:

A sample scene set up

To create this, we make a few cube entities and group them under an empty game object called **Obstacles**. We also create another cube object called `Agent` and give it our obstacle avoidance script. We then create a ground plane object to assist in finding a target position.

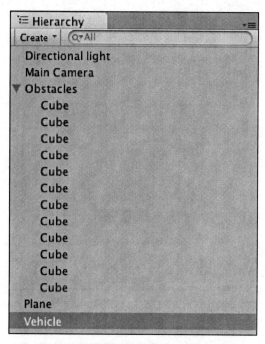

Here is how the Hierarchy is organized

It is worth noting that this `Agent` object is not a pathfinder. As such, if we set too many walls up, our `Agent` might have a hard time finding the target. Try a few wall setups and see how our `Agent` performs.

Adding a custom layer

We will now add a custom layer to our object. To add a new layer, we navigate to **Edit | Project Settings | Tags**. Assign the name `Obstacles` to **User Layer 8**. Now, we go back to our cube entity and set its `layer` property to `Obstacles`.

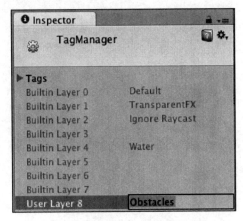

Creating a new layer

This is our new layer, which is added to Unity3D. Later, when we do the ray casting to detect obstacles, we'll only check for those entities using this particular layer. This way, we can ignore some objects that are not obstacles that are being hit by a ray, such as bushes or vegetation.

Assigning our new layer

For larger projects, our game objects probably already have a layer assigned to them. As such, instead of changing the object's layer to `Obstacles`, we would instead make a list using bitmaps of layers for our cube entity to use when detecting obstacles. We will talk more about bitmaps in the next section.

Layers are most commonly used by cameras to render a part of the scene and by lights to illuminate only some parts of the scene. But, they can also be used by ray casting to selectively ignore colliders or to create collisions. You can learn more about this at http://docs.unity3d. com/Documentation/Components/Layers.html.

Obstacle avoidance

Now it is time to make the script that will help our cube entity avoid those walls.

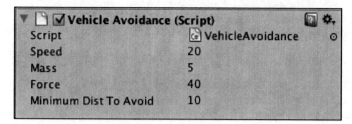

Properties of our Vehicle Avoidance script

As usual, we first initialize our entity script with the default properties and draw a GUI text in our OnGUI method. Let's take a look at the following code in the VehicleAvoidance.cs file:

```
using UnityEngine;
using System.Collections;

public class VehicleAvoidance : MonoBehaviour {
  public float speed = 20.0f;
  public float mass = 5.0f;
  public float force = 50.0f;
  public float minimumDistToAvoid = 20.0f;

  //Actual speed of the vehicle
  private float curSpeed;
  private Vector3 targetPoint;

  // Use this for initialization
  void Start () {
    mass = 5.0f;
    targetPoint = Vector3.zero;
  }

  void OnGUI() {
    GUILayout.Label("Click anywhere to move the vehicle.");
  }
```

Then in our Update method, we update the agent entity's position and rotation based on the direction vector returned by the AvoidObstacles method:

```
//Update is called once per frame
void Update () {
  //Vehicle move by mouse click
  RaycastHit hit;
```

```
var ray = Camera.main.ScreenPointToRay
    (Input.mousePosition);

if (Input.GetMouseButtonDown(0) &&
   Physics.Raycast(ray, out hit, 100.0f)) {
   targetPoint = hit.point;
}

//Directional vector to the target position
Vector3 dir = (targetPoint - transform.position);
dir.Normalize();

//Apply obstacle avoidance
AvoidObstacles(ref dir);

//...

}
```

The first thing we do in our `Update` method is retrieve the mouse click position so we can move our AI entity. We do this by shooting a ray from the camera in the direction it's looking. Then, we take the point where the ray hit the ground plane as our target position. Once we get the target position vector, we can calculate the direction vector by subtracting the current position vector from the target position vector. Then we call the `AvoidObstacles` method and pass in this direction vector:

```
//Calculate the new directional vector to avoid
   //the obstacle
public void AvoidObstacles(ref Vector3 dir) {
   RaycastHit hit;

   //Only detect layer 8 (Obstacles)
   int layerMask = 1<<8;

   //Check that the vehicle hit with the obstacles within
      //it's minimum distance to avoid
   if (Physics.Raycast(transform.position,
      transform.forward, out hit,
      minimumDistToAvoid, layerMask)) {
   //Get the normal of the hit point to calculate the
      //new direction
      Vector3 hitNormal = hit.normal;
      hitNormal.y = 0.0f; //Don't want to move in Y-Space
```

```
        //Get the new directional vector by adding force to
        //vehicle's current forward vector
      dir = transform.forward + hitNormal * force;
    }
  }
}
```

The `AvoidObstacles` method is also quite simple. The only trick to note here is that raycasting interacts selectively with the `Obstacles` layer that we specified at **User Layer 8** in our Unity3D **Tag Manager**. The `Raycast` method accepts a layer mask parameter to determine which layers to ignore and which to consider during raycasting. Now, if you look at how many layers you can specify in **Tag Manager**, you'll find a total of 32 layers. Therefore, Unity3D uses a 32-bit integer number to represent this layer mask parameter. For example, the following would represent a zero in 32 bits:

0000 0000 0000 0000 0000 0000 0000 0000

By default Unity3D uses the first eight layers as built-in layers. So, when you raycast without using a layer mask parameter, it'll raycast against all those eight layers, which could be represented like the following in a bitmask:

0000 0000 0000 0000 0000 0000 1111 1111

Our `Obstacles` layer was set at layer 8 (9th index), and we only want to raycast against this layer. So, we'd like to set up our bitmask in the following way:

0000 0000 0000 0000 0000 0001 0000 0000

The easiest way to set up this bitmask is by using the bit shift operators. We only need to place the 'on' bit or 1, at the 9th index, which means we can just move that bit 8 places to the left. So, we use the left shift operator to move the bit 8 places to the left, as shown in the following code:

```
int layerMask = 1<<8;
```

If we wanted to use multiple layer masks, say layer 8 and layer 9, an easy way would be to use the bitwise OR operator like this:

```
int layerMask = (1<<8) | (1<<9);
```

> You can also find a good discussion on using layermasks on Unity3D online. The question and answer site can be found at http://answers.unity3d.com/ questions/8715/how-do-i-use-layermasks.html.

Once we have the layer mask, we call the `Physics.Raycast` method from the current entity's position and in the forward direction. For the length of the ray, we use our `minimumDistToAvoid` variable so that we'll only avoid those obstacles that are being hit by the ray within this distance.

Then we take the normal vector of the hit ray, multiply it with the force vector, and add it to the current direction of our entity to get the new resultant direction vector, which we return from this method.

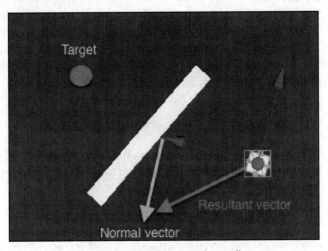

How our cube entity avoids a wall

Then in our `Update` method, we use this new direction after avoiding obstacles to rotate the AI entity and update the position according to the speed value.

```
void Update () {

    //...

    //Don't move the vehicle when the target point
      //is reached
    if (Vector3.Distance(targetPoint,
      transform.position) < 3.0f) return;

      //Assign the speed with delta time
      curSpeed = speed * Time.deltaTime;

      //Rotate the vehicle to its target
        //directional vector
```

```
var rot = Quaternion.LookRotation(dir);
transform.rotation = Quaternion.Slerp
  (transform.rotation, rot, 5.0f *
  Time.deltaTime);

  //Move the vehicle towards
    transform.position += transform.forward *
      curSpeed;
}
```

Summary

In this chapter, we set up two scenes and studied how to build path following agents together with obstacle avoidance behavior. We learned about the Unity3D layer feature and how to selectively raycast against a particular layer. Although the samples were simple, we can apply those simple techniques in various scenarios. For instance, we can set up a path along a road, and by using some vehicle models combined with obstacle avoidance behavior, we can easily set up a decent traffic simulation. Or you can just replace them with biped characters and build crowd simulation. You can also combine them with some finite states to add some more behaviors to make them more intelligent. This simple obstacle avoidance behavior that was implemented in this chapter doesn't consider the optimal path to reach the target position. Instead, it just goes straight to that target, and only if an obstacle is seen within a particular distance does it try to avoid it. It's supposed to be used among moving or dynamic objects and obstacles.

In the following chapter, we'll study how to implement a pathfinding algorithm called A* to determine the optimal path before moving, while avoiding static obstacles.

7
A* Pathfinding

In this chapter, we'll implement A* algorithm in Unity3D environment using C#. The A* pathfinding algorithm is widely used in games and interactive applications even though there are other algorithms, such as Dijkstra's algorithm, because of its simplicity and effectiveness. We've briefly covered this algorithm previously in *Chapter 1, Introduction to AI*. But let's review the algorithm again from an implementation perspective.

A* algorithm revisit

Let's review the A* algorithm again before we proceed to implement it in next section. First, we'll need to represent the map in a traversable data structure. While many structures are possible, for this example we will use a 2D grid array. We'll implement the GridManager class later to handle this map information. Our GridManager class will keep a list of the Node objects that are basically titles in a 2D grid. So we need to implement that Node class to handle things such as node type; whether it's a traversable node or an obstacle, cost to pass through and cost to reach the goal Node, and so on.

We'll have two variables to store the nodes that have been processed and the nodes that we have to process. We'll call them closed list and open list respectively. We'll implement that list type in the PriorityQueue class. And then finally, the following A* algorithm will be implemented in the AStar class. Let's take a look at it:

1. First, we start with the starting node and put it in the open list.
2. As long as the open list has some nodes in it, we'll perform the following process.
3. Pick the first node from the open list and keep it as the current node. (This is assuming that we've sorted the open list and the first node has the least cost value, which will be mentioned at the end of the code.)

4. Get the neighboring nodes of this current node, which are not obstacle types, such as a wall or canyon that can't be passed through.

5. For each neighbor node, check if this neighbor node is already in the closed list. If not we'll calculate the total cost (F) for this neighbor node using the following formula:

   ```
   F = G + H
   ```

   In the preceding formula, G is the total cost from the previous node to this node and H is the total cost from this node to the final target node.

6. Store that cost data in the neighbor node object. Also, store the current node as the parent node as well. Later we'll use this parent node data to trace back the actual path.

7. Put this neighbor node in the open list. Sort the open list in ascending order, ordered by the total cost to reach the target node.

8. If there's no more neighbor nodes to process, put the current node in the closed list and remove it from the open list.

9. Go back to step 2.

Once you have completed this process your current node should be in the target goal node position, but only if there's an obstacle free path to reach the goal node from the start node. If it is not at the goal node, then there's no available path to the target node from the current node position. If there's a valid path all we have to do now is to trace back from current node's parent node, until we reach the start node again. That'll give us a path list of all the nodes that we chose during our pathfinding process ordered from the target node to the start node. We then just reverse this path list, since we want to know the path from the start node to the target goal node.

This is a general overview of the algorithm we're going to implement in Unity3D using C#. So let's get started.

Implementation

We'll implement the preliminary classes that were mentioned before, such as the Node class, the GridManager class, and the PriorityQueue class. Then we'll use them in our main AStar class.

Node

The Node class will handle each tile object in our 2D grid representing the maps shown in the Node.cs file:

```csharp
using UnityEngine;
using System.Collections;
using System;

public class Node : IComparable {
    public float nodeTotalCost;
    public float estimatedCost;
    public bool bObstacle;
    public Node parent;
    public Vector3 position;

    public Node() {
        this.estimatedCost = 0.0f;
        this.nodeTotalCost = 1.0f;
        this.bObstacle = false;
        this.parent = null;
    }

    public Node(Vector3 pos) {
        this.estimatedCost = 0.0f;
        this.nodeTotalCost = 1.0f;
        this.bObstacle = false;
        this.parent = null;
        this.position = pos;
    }

    public void MarkAsObstacle() {
        this.bObstacle = true;
    }
```

The Node class has properties, such as the cost values (G and H), flags to mark whether it is an obstacle, its positions and parent node. The nodeTotalCost is G, which is the movement cost value from starting node to this node so far and the estimatedCost is H, which is total estimated cost from this node to the target goal node. We also have two simple constructor methods and a wrapper method to set whether this node is an obstacle. Then, we implement the CompareTo method as shown in the following code:

```csharp
public int CompareTo(object obj) {
    Node node = (Node)obj;
    //Negative value means object comes before this in the sort
      //order.
    if (this.estimatedCost < node.estimatedCost)
```

```
        return -1;
      //Positive value means object comes after this in the sort
        //order.
      if (this.estimatedCost > node.estimatedCost) return 1;
      return 0;
    }
  }
```

This method is important. Our `Node` class inherits from `IComparable` because we want to override this `CompareTo` method. If you can recall what we discussed in the previous algorithm section, you'll notice that we need to sort our list of node arrays based on the total estimated cost. The `ArrayList` type has a method called `Sort`. `Sort` basically looks for this `CompareTo` method, implemented inside the object (in this case our `Node` objects) from the list. So, we implement this method to sort the node objects based on our `estimatedCost` value. You can learn more about this .NET framework feature in the following resource.

The `IComparable.CompareTo` method can be found at `http://msdn.microsoft.com/en-us/library/system.icomparable.compareto.aspx`.

PriorityQueue

A `PriorityQueue` is a short and simple class to make the handling of the nodes, `ArrayList` easier as shown in the following `PriorityQueue.cs` class:

```
using UnityEngine;
using System.Collections;

public class PriorityQueue {
  private ArrayList nodes = new ArrayList();

  public int Length {
    get { return this.nodes.Count; }
  }

  public bool Contains(object node) {
    return this.nodes.Contains(node);
  }

  public Node First() {
    if (this.nodes.Count > 0) {
      return (Node)this.nodes[0];
    }
```

```
    return null;
  }

  public void Push(Node node) {
    this.nodes.Add(node);
    this.nodes.Sort();
  }

  public void Remove(Node node) {
    this.nodes.Remove(node);
    //Ensure the list is sorted
    this.nodes.Sort();
  }
}
```

The preceding code listing should be easy to understand. One thing to notice is that after adding or removing node from the nodes' ArrayList, we call the Sort method. This will call the Node object's CompareTo method, and will sort the nodes accordingly by the estimatedCost value.

GridManager

A GridManager class handles all the properties of the grid representing the map. We'll keep a singleton instance of the GridManager class, as we need only one object to represent the map, as shown in the following GridManager.cs file:

```
using UnityEngine;
using System.Collections;

public class GridManager : MonoBehaviour {
  private static GridManager s_Instance = null;

  public static GridManager instance {
    get {
      if (s_Instance == null) {
        s_Instance = FindObjectOfType(typeof(GridManager))
            as GridManager;
        if (s_Instance == null)
          Debug.Log("Could not locate a GridManager " +
              "object. \n You have to have exactly " +
              "one GridManager in the scene.");
      }
      return s_Instance;
    }
  }
```

We look for the `GridManager` object in our scene and if found, we keep it in our `s_Instance` static variable.

```
public int numOfRows;
public int numOfColumns;
public float gridCellSize;
public bool showGrid = true;
public bool showObstacleBlocks = true;

private Vector3 origin = new Vector3();
private GameObject[] obstacleList;
public Node[,] nodes { get; set; }
public Vector3 Origin {
  get { return origin; }
}
```

Next, we declare all the variables; we'll need to represent our map, such as number of rows and columns, the size of each grid tile, and some boolean variables to visualize the grid and obstacles as well as to store all the nodes present in the grid as shown in the following code:

```
void Awake() {
  obstacleList = GameObject.FindGameObjectsWithTag("Obstacle");
  CalculateObstacles();
}
// Find all the obstacles on the map
void CalculateObstacles() {
  nodes = new Node[numOfColumns, numOfRows];
  int index = 0;
  for (int i = 0; i < numOfColumns; i++) {
    for (int j = 0; j < numOfRows; j++) {
      Vector3 cellPos = GetGridCellCenter(index);
      Node node = new Node(cellPos);
      nodes[i, j] = node;
      index++;
    }
  }
  if (obstacleList != null && obstacleList.Length > 0) {
    //For each obstacle found on the map, record it in our list
    foreach (GameObject data in obstacleList) {
      int indexCell = GetGridIndex(data.transform.position);
      int col = GetColumn(indexCell);
      int row = GetRow(indexCell);
      nodes[row, col].MarkAsObstacle();
    }
  }
}
```

We look for all the game objects with a tag `Obstacle` and put them in our `obstacleList` property. Then we set up our nodes' 2D array in the `CalculateObstacles` method. First, we just create the normal node objects with default properties. Just after that we examine our `obstacleList`. Convert their position into row, column data and update the nodes at that index to be obstacles.

The `GridManager` has a couple of helper methods to traverse the grid and get the grid cell data. The following are some of them with a brief description of what they do. The implementation is simple, so we won't go into the details.

The `GetGridCellCenter` method returns the position of the grid cell in world coordinates from the cell index, as shown in the following code:

```
public Vector3 GetGridCellCenter(int index) {
  Vector3 cellPosition = GetGridCellPosition(index);
  cellPosition.x += (gridCellSize / 2.0f);
  cellPosition.z += (gridCellSize / 2.0f);
  return cellPosition;
}

public Vector3 GetGridCellPosition(int index) {
  int row = GetRow(index);
  int col = GetColumn(index);
  float xPosInGrid = col * gridCellSize;
  float zPosInGrid = row * gridCellSize;
  return Origin + new Vector3(xPosInGrid, 0.0f, zPosInGrid);
}
```

The `GetGridIndex` method returns the grid cell index in the grid from the given position:

```
public int GetGridIndex(Vector3 pos) {
  if (!IsInBounds(pos)) {
    return -1;
  }
  pos -= Origin;
  int col = (int)(pos.x / gridCellSize);
  int row = (int)(pos.z / gridCellSize);
  return (row * numOfColumns + col);
}

public bool IsInBounds(Vector3 pos) {
  float width = numOfColumns * gridCellSize;
  float height = numOfRows* gridCellSize;
  return (pos.x >= Origin.x &&  pos.x <= Origin.x + width &&
      pos.x <= Origin.z + height && pos.z >= Origin.z);
}
```

The GetRow and GetColumn methods return the row and column data of the grid cell from the given index:

```
public int GetRow(int index) {
    int row = index / numOfColumns;
    return row;
}

public int GetColumn(int index) {
    int col = index % numOfColumns;
    return col;
}
```

Another important method is GetNeighbours, which is used by the AStar class to retrieve the neighboring nodes of a particular node:

```
public void GetNeighbours(Node node, ArrayList neighbors) {
    Vector3 neighborPos = node.position;
    int neighborIndex = GetGridIndex(neighborPos);

    int row = GetRow(neighborIndex);
    int column = GetColumn(neighborIndex);

    //Bottom
    int leftNodeRow = row - 1;
    int leftNodeColumn = column;
    AssignNeighbour(leftNodeRow, leftNodeColumn, neighbors);

    //Top
    leftNodeRow = row + 1;
    leftNodeColumn = column;
    AssignNeighbour(leftNodeRow, leftNodeColumn, neighbors);

    //Right
    leftNodeRow = row;
    leftNodeColumn = column + 1;
    AssignNeighbour(leftNodeRow, leftNodeColumn, neighbors);

    //Left
    leftNodeRow = row;
    leftNodeColumn = column - 1;
    AssignNeighbour(leftNodeRow, leftNodeColumn, neighbors);
}
```

```
void AssignNeighbour(int row, int column, ArrayList neighbors) {
  if (row != -1 && column != -1 &&
      row < numOfRows && column < numOfColumns) {
    Node nodeToAdd = nodes[row, column];
    if (!nodeToAdd.bObstacle) {
      neighbors.Add(nodeToAdd);
    }
  }
}
```

First, we retrieve the neighboring nodes of the current node in the left, right, top, and bottom four directions. Then, inside the `AssignNeighbour` method, we check the node to see whether it's an obstacle. If it's not then we push that neighbor node to the referenced array list, `neighbors`. The next method is a debug aid method to visualize the grid and obstacle blocks.

```
void OnDrawGizmos() {
  if (showGrid) {
    DebugDrawGrid(transform.position, numOfRows, numOfColumns,
        gridCellSize, Color.blue);
  }
  Gizmos.DrawSphere(transform.position, 0.5f);
  if (showObstacleBlocks) {
    Vector3 cellSize = new Vector3(gridCellSize, 1.0f,
      gridCellSize);
    if (obstacleList != null && obstacleList.Length > 0) {
      foreach (GameObject data in obstacleList) {
        Gizmos.DrawCube(GetGridCellCenter(
            GetGridIndex(data.transform.position)), cellSize);
      }
    }
  }
}

public void DebugDrawGrid(Vector3 origin, int numRows, int
  numCols,float cellSize, Color color) {
  float width = (numCols * cellSize);
  float height = (numRows * cellSize);

  // Draw the horizontal grid lines
  for (int i = 0; i < numRows + 1; i++) {
    Vector3 startPos = origin + i * cellSize * new Vector3(0.0f,
      0.0f, 1.0f);
    Vector3 endPos = startPos + width * new Vector3(1.0f, 0.0f,
      0.0f);
    Debug.DrawLine(startPos, endPos, color);
  }
```

```
        // Draw the vertial grid lines
        for (int i = 0; i < numCols + 1; i++) {
          Vector3 startPos = origin + i * cellSize * new Vector3(1.0f,
              0.0f, 0.0f);
          Vector3 endPos = startPos + height * new Vector3(0.0f, 0.0f,
              1.0f);
          Debug.DrawLine(startPos, endPos, color);
        }
      }
    }
```

Gizmos can be used to draw visual debugging and setup aids inside the editor scene view. OnDrawGizmos is called every frame by the engine. So, if the debug flags, showGrid and showObstacleBlocks are checked, we just draw the grid with lines and obstacle cube objects with cubes. Let's not go through the DebugDrawGrid method, which is quite simple.

You can learn more about gizmos in the following Unity3D reference documentation at http://docs.unity3d.com/Documentation/ScriptReference/Gizmos.html.

AStar

The AStar class is the main class that will utilize the classes we have implemented so far. You can go back to the algorithm section, if you want to review this. We start with our openList and closedList declarations which are of the PriorityQueue type as shown in the AStar.cs file:

```
using UnityEngine;
using System.Collections;

public class AStar {
    public static PriorityQueue closedList, openList;
```

Next we implement a method called HeuristicEstimateCost to calculate the cost between the two nodes. The calculation is simple. We just find the direction vector between the two by subtracting one position vector from another. The magnitude of this resultant vector gives the direct distance from the current node to the goal node.

```
    private static float HeuristicEstimateCost(Node curNode,
        Node goalNode) {
      Vector3 vecCost = curNode.position - goalNode.position;
      return vecCost.magnitude;
    }
```

Next, we have our main `FindPath` method:

```
public static ArrayList FindPath(Node start, Node goal) {
  openList = new PriorityQueue();
  openList.Push(start);
  start.nodeTotalCost = 0.0f;
  start.estimatedCost = HeuristicEstimateCost(start, goal);

  closedList = new PriorityQueue();
  Node node = null;
```

We initialize our open and closed lists. Starting with the start node, we put it in our open list. Then we start processing our open list.

```
  while (openList.Length != 0) {
    node = openList.First();
    //Check if the current node is the goal node
    if (node.position == goal.position) {
      return CalculatePath(node);
    }

    //Create an ArrayList to store the neighboring nodes
    ArrayList neighbours = new ArrayList();

    GridManager.instance.GetNeighbours(node, neighbours);

    for (int i = 0; i < neighbours.Count; i++) {
      Node neighbourNode = (Node)neighbours[i];

      if (!closedList.Contains(neighbourNode)) {
        float cost = HeuristicEstimateCost(node,
            neighbourNode);

        float totalCost = node.nodeTotalCost + cost;
        float neighbourNodeEstCost = HeuristicEstimateCost(
            neighbourNode, goal);

        neighbourNode.nodeTotalCost = totalCost;
        neighbourNode.parent = node;
        neighbourNode.estimatedCost = totalCost +
            neighbourNodeEstCost;

        if (!openList.Contains(neighbourNode)) {
          openList.Push(neighbourNode);
        }
      }
    }
  }
```

```
      //Push the current node to the closed list
      closedList.Push(node);
      //and remove it from openList
      openList.Remove(node);
  }

  if (node.position != goal.position) {
    Debug.LogError("Goal Not Found");
    return null;
  }
  return CalculatePath(node);
}
```

This code implementation resembles the algorithm that we have previously discussed, so you can refer back to it, if you are not clear of certain things.

1. Get the first node of our `openList`. Remember our `openList` of nodes is always sorted every time a new node is added. So the first node is always the node with the least estimated cost to the goal node.

2. Check if the current node is already at the goal node. If so, exit the `while` loop and build the `path` array.

3. Create an array list to store the neighboring nodes of the current node being processed. Use the `GetNeighbours` method to retrieve the neighbors from the grid.

4. For every node in the neighbors array, we check if it's already in the `closedList`. If not, put it in the calculate the cost values, update the node properties with the new cost values as well as the parent node data and put it in `openList`.

5. Push the current node to `closedList` and remove it from `openList`. Go back to step 1.

If there are no more nodes in `openList`, our current node should be at the target node if there's a valid path available. Then we just call the `CalculatePath` method with the current node parameter.

```
private static ArrayList CalculatePath(Node node) {
  ArrayList list = new ArrayList();
  while (node != null) {
    list.Add(node);
    node = node.parent;
  }
  list.Reverse();
  return list;
}
}
```

The `CalculatePath` method traces through each node's parent node object and builds an array list. It gives an array list with nodes from target node to start node. Since we want a path array from start node to target node we just call the `Reverse` method.

So this is our `AStar` class. We'll write a test script in the following code to test all this. Then set up a scene to use them in.

TestCode class

This class will use the `AStar` class to find the path from the start node to the goal node as shown in the following `TestCode.cs` file:

```
using UnityEngine;
using System.Collections;

public class TestCode : MonoBehaviour {
   private Transform startPos, endPos;
   public Node startNode { get; set; }
   public Node goalNode { get; set; }

   public ArrayList pathArray;

   GameObject objStartCube, objEndCube;
   private float elapsedTime = 0.0f;
   //Interval time between pathfinding

   public float intervalTime = 1.0f;
```

First we set up the variables that we'll need to reference. The `pathArray` is to store the nodes array returned from the `AStar FindPath` method.

```
   void Start () {
     objStartCube = GameObject.FindGameObjectWithTag("Start");
     objEndCube = GameObject.FindGameObjectWithTag("End");

     pathArray = new ArrayList();
     FindPath();
   }

   void Update () {
     elapsedTime += Time.deltaTime;
     if (elapsedTime >= intervalTime) {
       elapsedTime = 0.0f;
       FindPath();
     }
   }
}
```

In the `Start` method we look for objects with the tags `Start` and `End`, and initialize our `pathArray` as well. We'll be trying to find our new path at every interval that we set to our `intervalTime` property in case the positions of the start and end nodes have changed. Then we call the `FindPath` method.

```
void FindPath() {
  startPos = objStartCube.transform;
  endPos = objEndCube.transform;

  startNode = new Node(GridManager.instance.GetGridCellCenter(
      GridManager.instance.GetGridIndex(startPos.position)));

  goalNode = new Node(GridManager.instance.GetGridCellCenter(
      GridManager.instance.GetGridIndex(endPos.position)));

  pathArray = AStar.FindPath(startNode, goalNode);
}
```

Since we implemented our pathfinding algorithm in the `AStar` class, finding a path has now become a lot simpler. First, we take the positions of our start and end game objects. Then, we create new `Node` objects using the helper methods of `GridManager`, `GetGridIndex`, to calculate their respective row and column index positions inside the grid. Once we get that we just call the `AStar.FindPath` method with the start node and goal node, and store the returned array list in the local `pathArray` property. Next we implement the `OnDrawGizmos` method to draw and visualize the path found.

```
void OnDrawGizmos() {
  if (pathArray == null)
    return;

  if (pathArray.Count > 0) {
    int index = 1;
    foreach (Node node in pathArray) {
      if (index < pathArray.Count) {
        Node nextNode = (Node)pathArray[index];
        Debug.DrawLine(node.position, nextNode.position,
          Color.green);
        index++;
      }
    }
  }
}
```

We look through our `pathArray` and use the `Debug.DrawLine` method to draw the lines connecting the nodes from the `pathArray`. With that we'll be able to see a green line connecting the nodes from start to end forming a path, when we run and test our program.

Scene setup

We are going to setup a scene that looks something similar to the following screenshot:

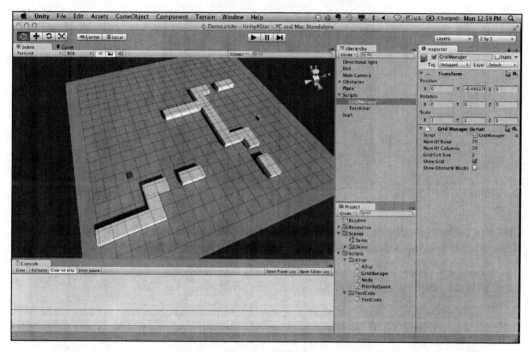

Sample test scene

We'll have a directional light, the start and end game objects, a few obstacle objects, a plane entity to be used as ground and two empty game objects in which to put our **GridManager** and **TestAStar** scripts. This is our scene hierarchy:

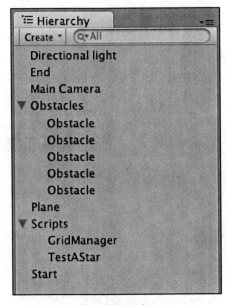

Scene hierarchy

Create a bunch of cube entities and tag them as Obstacle. We'll be looking for objects with this tag when running our pathfinding algorithm.

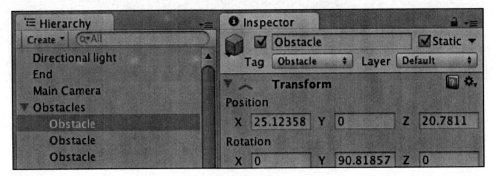

Obstacle nodes

Create a cube entity and tag it as `Start`.

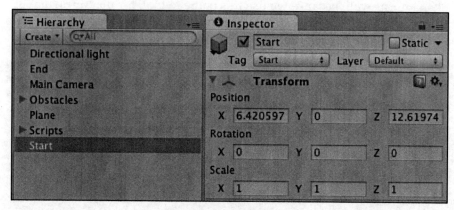

Start node

Then create another cube entity and tag it as `End`.

End node

Now create an empty game object and attach the **GridManager** script. Set the name as GridManager as well, because we use this name to look for the GridManager object from our script. Here we can setup the number of rows and columns for our grid as well as the size of each tile.

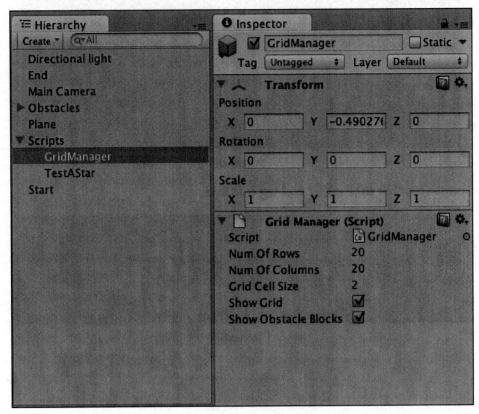

GridManager script

Testing

Let's hit the **Play** button and see our A* pathfinding algorithm in action. By default, once you play the scene Unity3D will switch to the **Game** view. Since our pathfinding visualization code is written for debug draw in the editor view, you'll need to switch back to the **Scene** view or enable **Gizmos** to see the path found.

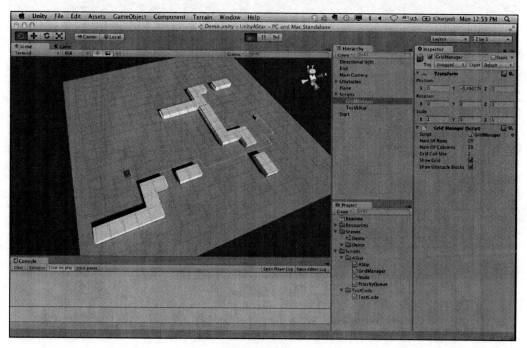

Found path one

Now try to move the start or end node around in the scene using the editor's movement gizmo. (Not in the **Game** view, but the **Scene** view.)

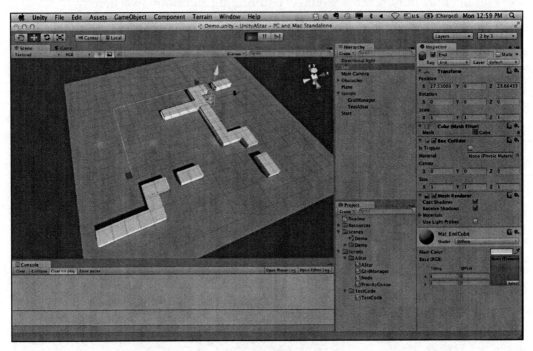

Found path two

You should see the path updated accordingly if there's a valid path from the start node to the target goal node, dynamically in real-time. You'll get an error message in the console window if there's no available path.

Summary

In this chapter, we learned how to implement the A* pathfinding algorithm in the Unity3D environment. We implemented our own A* pathfinding class as well as our own grid class, queue class, and node class. We learnt about the IComparable interface and overriding the CompareTo method. We used debug draw functionalities to visualize the grid and path formation. With Unity3D's navmesh and navagent features it may not be necessary for you to implement this pathfinding algorithm on your own. Nonetheless, it helps you to understand the underlying algorithm behind the implementation.

In the next chapter, we will look at how to extend the idea behind A* and look at navigation meshes. With navigation meshes, it will be much easier for us to find a path over uneven terrain.

8
Navigation Mesh

In this chapter, we'll learn how to use Unity's built-in navigation mesh generator that can make path finding for AI agents a lot easier. Unfortunately, this feature is only available in Unity Pro, so you need to have a license. Or, you can start using the 30-days free trial of Unity Pro (if you have not done so already) to follow along with the exercises in this chapter. To activate your free trial, navigate to **Unity | Manage License...**, and select **Activate new license**. Check the 30-day free trial option then click **OK**, and you should be good to go.

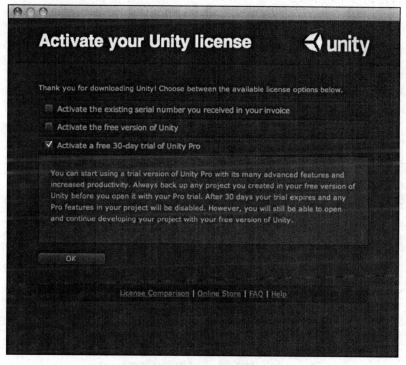

Activating free trial of Unity Pro

Introduction

AI path finding needs representation of the scene in a particular format. We've seen that using a 2D grid (array) for A* path finding on a 2D map. AI agents need to know where the obstacles are, especially the static obstacles. Dealing with collision avoidance between dynamically moving objects is another subject, primarily known as steering behaviors. Unity has a built-in navigation feature to generate a **navigation mesh** (**navmesh**) that represents the scene in a context that makes sense for our AI agents to find the optimum path to the target. This chapter comes with a Unity project that has four scenes in it. You should open it in Unity and see how it works to get a feeling of what we are going to build. Using this sample project, we'll study how to create a navmesh, and use it with AI agents inside our own scenes.

Setting up the map

To get started, we'll build a simple scene, as shown in the following figure. This is the first scene in our sample project called `NavMesh01-Simple.scene`. You can use a plane as a ground object and several cube entities as the wall objects. Later, we'll put in some AI agents (of course, our all time favorite tanks) to go to the mouse-clicked position, as in an RTS game.

Scene with obstacles—NavMesh01-Simple.scene

Navigation Static

Once we've added the walls and ground, it's important to mark them as **Navigation Static**, so that the navmesh generator knows those are the static obstacle objects to avoid. To do this, select all those objects, click on the **Static** button, and choose **Navigation Static**, as shown in the following figure.

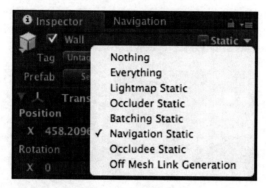

The Navigation Static property

Baking the navigation mesh

Now we're done with our scene. Let's bake the navmesh. Firstly, we need to open the navigation window. Navigate to **Window | Navigation**, and you should be able to see a window like this:

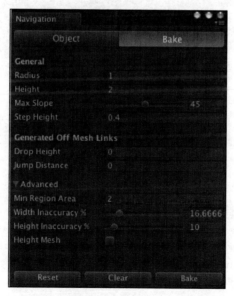

Navigation window

All these properties are pretty much self-explanatory and you can check out the following Unity reference documentation to learn more:

`http://docs.unity3d.com/Documentation/Manual/Navmeshbaking.html`

For now, we'll leave with the default values and just click on **Bake**. You should see a progress bar baking the navmesh for your scene, and after a while you'll see your navmesh in your scene, as shown in following diagram.

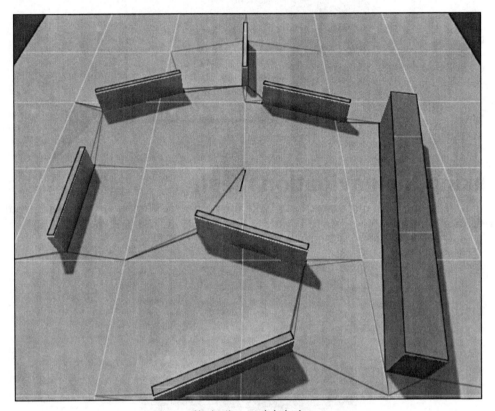

Navigation mesh baked

Nav Mesh Agent

We're pretty much done with setting up our super simple scene. Now, let's add some AI agents to see if it works. We'll use our tank model here. But if you're working with your own scene and don't have this model, you can just put a cube or a sphere entity as an agent. It'll work the same way.

Tank entity

The next step is to add the **Nav Mesh Agent** component to our tank entity. This component makes path finding really easy. We don't need to deal with path finding algorithms like A* anymore. By just setting the `destination` property of the component during runtime, our AI agent will automatically find the path itself.

Navigate to **Component | Navigation | Nav Mesh Agent** to add this component.

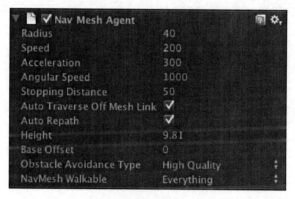

Nav Mesh Agent properties

 Unity reference for Nav Mesh Agent component can be found at `http://docs.unity3d.com/Documentation/Components/class-NavMeshAgent.html`

One property to note is the `NavMesh Walkable` property. This specifies the navmesh layers that this navmesh agent can walk. We'll talk about navigation layers in the *NavMeshLayers* section.

Updating agents' destinations

Now we've set up our AI agent, we need a way to tell this agent where to go and update the destination of our tanks to the mouse-click position.

So, let's add a sphere entity to be used as a marker object, and then attach the following `Target.cs` script to an empty game object. Drag-and-drop this sphere entity onto this script's `targetMarker` transform property in the inspector.

The Target.cs class

This is a simple class that does three things:

- Gets the mouse-click position using a ray
- Updates the marker position
- Updates the destination property of all the navmesh agents

The following lines show the code present in this class:

```
using UnityEngine;
using System.Collections;

public class Target : MonoBehaviour {
  private NavMeshAgent[] navAgents;
  public Transform targetMarker;

  void Start() {
    navAgents = FindObjectsOfType(typeof(NavMeshAgent)) as
        NavMeshAgent[];
  }

  void UpdateTargets(Vector3 targetPosition) {
    foreach (NavMeshAgent agent in navAgents) {
      agent.destination = targetPosition;
    }
  }

  void Update() {
    int button = 0;

    //Get the point of the hit position when the mouse is
    //being clicked
    if(Input.GetMouseButtonDown(button)) {
      Ray ray = Camera.main.ScreenPointToRay(
          Input.mousePosition);

      RaycastHit hitInfo;
```

```
if (Physics.Raycast(ray.origin, ray.direction,
        out hitInfo)) {
    Vector3 targetPosition = hitInfo.point;
    UpdateTargets(targetPosition);
    targetMarker.position = targetPosition +
        new Vector3(0,5,0);
        }
    }
  }
}
```

At the start of the game, we look for all the `NavMeshAgent` type entities in our game and store them in our reference `NavMeshAgent` array. Whenever there's a mouse-click event, we do a simple raycast to determine the first objects that collide with our ray. If the ray hits any object, we update the position of our marker and update each navmesh agent's destination by setting the destination property with the new position. We'll be using this script throughout this chapter to tell the destination position for our AI agents.

Now, test run the scene, and click on a point where you want your tanks to go. The tanks should come as close as possible to that point while avoiding the static obstacles like walls.

Scene with slope

Let's build a scene with some slopes like this:

Scene with slopes—NavMesh02-Slope.scene

One important thing to note is that the slopes and the wall should be in contact with each other. Objects need to be perfectly connected when creating such joints in the scene with the purpose of generating a navmesh later. Otherwise, there'll be gaps in navmesh and the agents will not be able to find the path anymore. There's a feature called Off Mesh Links generation to solve this kind of problem. We'll look at Off Mesh Links in the *Off Mesh Links* section later in this chapter. For now, make sure to connect the slope properly.

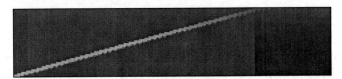

A well-connected slope

Next, we can adjust the `Max Slope` property in the **Navigation** window's **Bake** tab according to the level of slope in our scenes that we want to allow agents to travel. We'll use `45` degrees here. If your slopes are steeper than this, you can use a higher `Max Slope` value.

Max Slope property

Bake the scene, and you should have a navmesh generated like this:

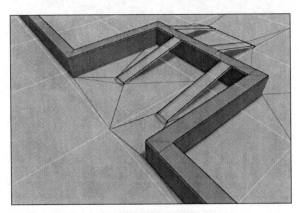

Nav Mesh generated

Next, we'll place some tanks with the **Nav Mesh Agent** component. Create a new cube object to be used as a target reference position. We'll be using our previous `Target.cs` script to update the destination property of our AI agent. Test run the scene, and you should have your AI agents crossing the slopes to reach the target.

NavMeshLayers

In games with complex environments, we usually have some areas that are harder to travel in than others, such as a pond or a lake compared to crossing a bridge. Even though it could be the shortest path to target by crossing the pond directly, we would want our agents to choose the bridge as it makes more sense. In other words, we want to make crossing the pond to be more navigationally expensive than using the bridge. In this section, we'll look at NavMeshLayers, a way to define different layers with different navigation cost values.

We're going to build a scene as shown in the following figure. There'll be three planes to represent two ground planes connected with a bridge-like structure and a water plane between them. As you can see, it's the shortest path for our tank to cross over the water plane to reach our cube target. But we want our AI agents to choose the bridge if possible and to cross the water plane only if absolutely necessary, such as when the target object is on the water plane.

Scene with layers—NavMesh03-Layers.scene

The scene hierarchy can be seen in the following screenshot. Our game level is composed of planes, slopes, and walls. We've a tank entity and a destination cube with the Target.cs script attached.

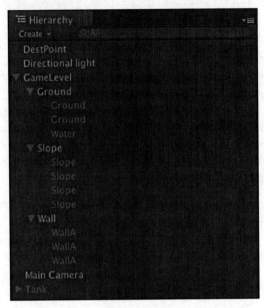

Scene hierarchy

To create your own NavMeshLayer, navigate to **Edit** | **Project Settings** | **NavMeshLayers**.

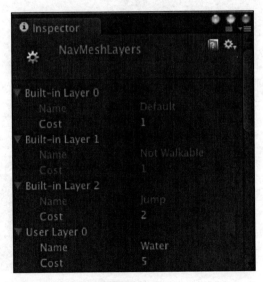

NavMeshLayers

Unity reference for Nav Mesh Layers can be found at
`http://docs.unity3d.com/Documentation/`
`Components/class-NavMeshLayers.html`

Unity comes with three default layers: `Default`, `Not Walkable`, and `Jump`, each with potentially different cost values. Let's add a new layer called `Water` and give it a cost of `5`.

Next, select the water plane. Go to the **Navigation** window and under the **Object** tab, set **Navigation Layer** to `Water`.

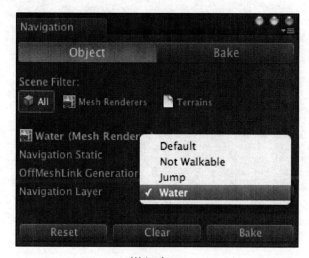

Water layer

Bake the navmesh for the scene, and run it to test it. You should see that the AI agents now choose the slope rather than going through the plane marked as the water layer because it's more expensive to choose that path. Try experimenting with placing the target object at different points in the water plane. You will see that the AI agents will sometimes swim back to the shore and take the bridge, rather than trying to swim all the way across the water.

Off Mesh Links

Sometimes there could be some gaps inside the scene that can make the navigation meshes disconnected. For example, our agents will not be able to find the path if our slopes are not connected to the walls in our previous examples. Or we could have set up points where our agents could jump off the wall and onto the plane below. Unity has a feature called **Off Mesh Links** to connect such gaps. Off Mesh Links can either be set up manually, or generated automatically by Unity's navmesh generator.

Here's the example scene that we're going to build in this example. As you can see, there's a small gap between the two planes. Let's see how to connect these two planes using Off Mesh Links.

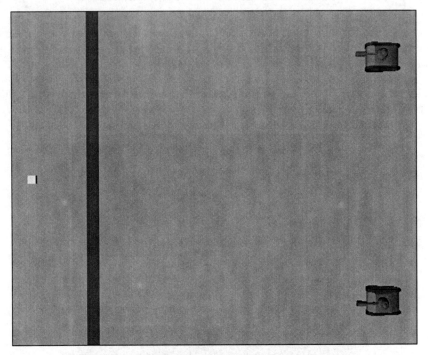

Scene with off mesh links—NavMesh04-OffMeshLinks.scene

Generated Off Mesh Links

Firstly, we'll use autogenerated Off Mesh Links to connect the two planes. The first thing to do is to mark these two planes as Off Mesh Link Generation static in the property inspector, as shown in the following screenshot:

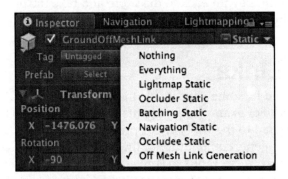

Off Mesh Link Generation static

Go to the **Navigation** window, and notice the following properties under the **Bake** tab. You can set the distance threshold to autogenerate Off Mesh Links.

Generated Off Mesh Links	
Drop Height	0
Jump Distance	50

Generated Off Mesh Links properties

Click on **Bake**, and you should have Off Mesh Links connecting two planes like this:

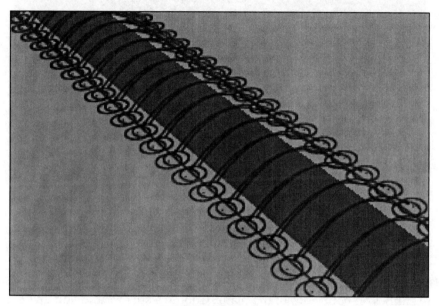

Generated Off Mesh Links

Now our AI agents can traverse and find the path across both planes. Agents will be essentially teleported to the other plane, once they have reached the edge of the plane and found the Off Mesh Link. Of course, if teleporting agents are not what we want, we had better put a bridge in for the agents to cross.

Manual Off Mesh Links

If we don't want to generate Off Mesh Links along the edge, and we want to force the agents to come to a certain point to be teleported to another plane, we can also manually set up the Off Mesh Links. Here's how:

Manual Off Mesh Links setup

This is our scene with a significant gap between two planes. We placed two pairs of sphere entities on both sides of the plane. Choose a sphere, and add an Off Mesh Link by navigating to **Component | Navigation | Off Mesh Link**. We only need to add this component on one sphere. Next, drag-and-drop the first sphere to the Start property, and the other sphere to the End property.

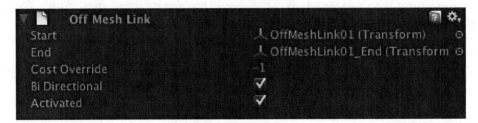

Off Mesh Link component

Unity reference for Off Mesh Links can be found at
`http://docs.unity3d.com/Documentation/`
`Components/class-OffMeshLink.html.`

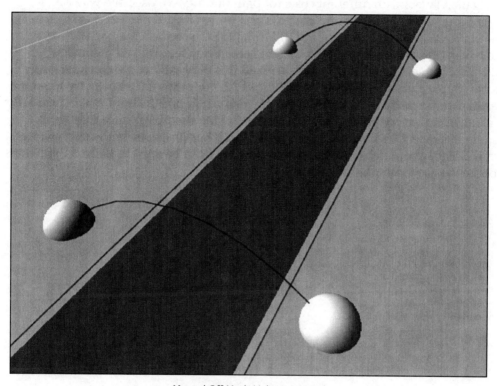

Manual Off Mesh Links generated

Go to the **Navigation** window and bake the scene. The planes are now connected with the manual Off Mesh Links that can be used by AI agents to traverse even though there's a gap.

Summary

In this chapter, we learned how to generate and use navigation meshes to represent the scene for path finding purposes. We studied how to set up different navigation layers with different costs for path finding. We used the **Nav Mesh Agent** component to easily find the path and move toward the target using the `destination` property. We set up Off Mesh Links to connect the gaps between the navigation meshes using both the autogeneration feature and manual set up with the Off Mesh Link component. With all this information, we can now easily create simple games with fairly complicated AI. For example, you can try to set the destination property of AI tanks to the player's tank's position and make them follow it. And, using simple FSMs, they can start attacking the player once they reach a certain distance. Our FSM has taken us far, but it has its limits. In the next chapter, we will learn about Behavior Trees, and how they can be used to make AI decisions in even the most complex of games.

9
Behavior Trees

Behavior trees are another way of controlling states and behaviors of our game characters. They are also an alternative to **finite state machines (FSMs)**, which was described in *Chapter 2, Finite State Machines*. Even though FSMs are simple to implement, intuitive, and easy to understand, it's hard to maintain and scale once the logic becomes too complex. One of the reasons for this is that in state machines, all the transitions between states have to be precisely defined. So, as the size of state machine becomes bigger, updating the structure of a state machine with all the transitions becomes extremely complex. So AI developers have moved on to find new ways and other techniques, such as **hierarchical FSM (HFSM)** and **Hierarchical Task Networks (HTNs)**. Behavior trees are one of them that have become popular with the use of AAA games such as Halo, Crysis, and Spore.

Since this book is focused on implementing AI in Unity3D, we won't cover implementing the whole behavior tree system from scratch. Luckily there's a powerful plugin called Behave for Unity3D to implement behavior trees. So we'll be using this in this chapter as well as studying the general components and ideas of behavior trees while implementing simple demos.

Behave plugin

Behave is a system for Unity3D to design game objects' behavior logic using behavior trees. It was designed and developed by *Emil Johansen* ("AngryAnt") who's currently working at Unity Technologies. The Behave system comes with a simple and easy to use drag-and-drop logic designer. Game designers can use this interface to set up the behavior logic while the developers implement the real actions. Since it's the easiest toolset to implement behavior trees in Unity3D, we'll be using this system to implement the agents' behaviors in this chapter.

The following are the steps to be performed for downloading and installing Behave:

1. First, let's go and download Behave from Unity Asset Store. Inside Unity3D, navigate to **Window | Asset Store**, and then search for behave.

2. Once you find **Behave**, click on the arrow beside the **Download** button and choose **Download and Import**. This will download the Behave system and import it into your currently opened Unity3D project. The latest version of Behave is Version 1.4, and is free. So, we'll be using this version. If you're using an earlier version, there could be minor or major changes and the code may not work out of the box.

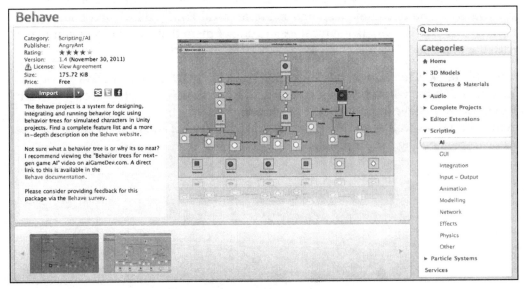

Behave on the Asset Store

3. Once you've imported Behave into your project you will see a folder called **Behave** in your project directory.

Behave library imported

You don't really need to worry about any of the contents of this folder. Once it's there we are ready to use the system.

Workflow

We'll briefly look at the general workflow of using Behave to implement behavior trees. After we look at how each component works individually, we will put the pieces together and build a demo involving robots and aliens. Let's get started by performing the following steps:

1. To use the Behave system, we first need to create a Behave library. So let's create one now, and call it **AgentBehaveLib**.

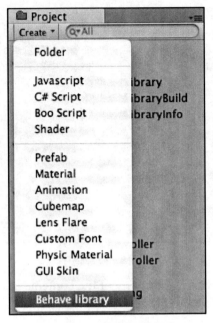

Create a new Behave library

2. Select your newly created **AgentBehaveLib** Behave library and click on **Edit library** from the property inspector.

A Behave library properties

3. The Behave browser panel will show up as shown in the following screenshot. Here you can create collections that hold actual behavior trees.

Create new collection

4. Create a new collection. Leave the default name. Then, while this collection is selected, create a new tree. Leave the default name here as well. Your **Behave browser** should look similar to the following screenshot:

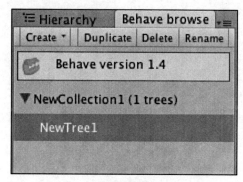

Behave browser

5. Select the behavior tree you just created and the **Behave editor** window should look something similar to the following screenshot. If you can't see the editor, navigate to **Window | Behave tree editor** to make it active.

There are six basic elements in creating behavior trees. It's best to use a tutorial style to study them. So, let's get started with the action nodes.

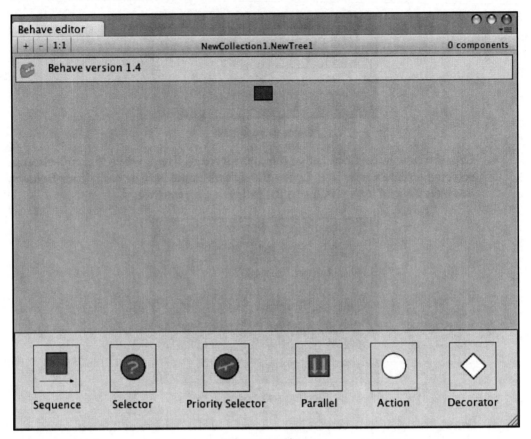

Behave tree editor

Action

Actions are the most basic nodes that actually execute something in behavior trees. Let's create a new action by dragging the action node into the Behave editor. Then link it up with the root node by clicking and dragging the root node until the link hooks into the top box of the action node. With the action node selected, rename the action from the Inspector to **MyAction** as shown in the following screenshot. This setup basically tells the Behave system that this behavior tree will execute this action a fixed number of times in a second (as provided in the **Frequency** variable of the node property). Make sure you set the frequency value to something besides zero, so that the functions we create later will actually be called. You can also find additional class reference information inside the property inspector panel.

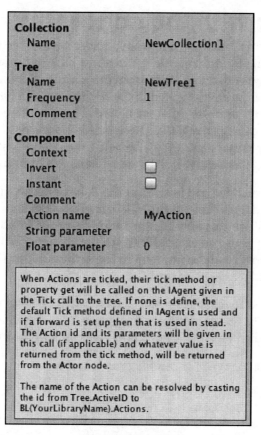

Collection
Name   NewCollection1

Tree
Name   NewTree1
Frequency   1
Comment

Component
Context
Invert   ☐
Instant   ☐
Comment
Action name   MyAction
String parameter
Float parameter   0

When Actions are ticked, their tick method or property get will be called on the IAgent given in the Tick call to the tree. If none is define, the default Tick method defined in IAgent is used and if a forward is set up then that is used in stead. The Action id and its parameters will be given in this call (if applicable) and whatever value is returned from the tick method, will be returned from the Actor node.

The name of the Action can be resolved by casting the id from Tree.ActiveID to BL(YourLibraryName).Actions.

Action node properties

If you set up the action node properties accordingly, your tree diagram should look something, as shown in the following screenshot:

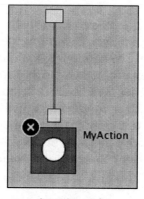

An action node

Interfacing with the script

Before we can access this behavior tree from a script we need to build or compile this behavior tree. Behave will compile the tree to a DLL so that we can reference and implement our own custom actions from our scripts. It is important to note that whenever we change anything inside the library, we will have to recompile the library before we try and use what we added. There are two options to build a Behave library either debug or release. These build options only apply to our Behave library and not to our actual game. We'll be using the debug build in this tutorial that will allow us to debug our behavior trees using Behave's built-in visual debugger.

So, to compile your behavior tree just select the Behave library (in this case `AgentBehaveLib`) and then click on **Build library debug** from the inspector panel. After a moment you'll see two new files are added to your project directory. You might need to refresh your project folder to see the changes. With that successfully built library we are now ready to implement the actions in our script. So let's create a new C# script and call it `AgentController`.

The first thing we need to do is to import Behave runtime library which can be found under the `Behave.Runtime` namespace. And we need to implement the `IAgent` interface defined by the Behave system so that we can handle our own actions.

The code in the `AgentController.cs` file is as follows:

```
using UnityEngine;
using System.Collections;
using Behave.Runtime;
using Tree = Behave.Runtime.Tree;

public class AgentController : MonoBehaviour, IAgent {

    Tree m_Tree;
```

Then we declare a `Tree` variable to reference our behavior tree. Then inside our `Start` method, we use the `InstantiateTree` static method of our library to create an instance of our behavior tree. The `BLAgentBehaveLib` library is generated by Behave using this naming pattern, `BL{YourLibraryName}`. Behave uses that kind of naming convention, as you will see later, and it's important to keep the names the way it needs. The `InstantiateTree` method accepts two parameters: the tree type to instantiate and the reference to a class that implements the `IAgent` interface, in our case we just pass in this to refer the current class. Notice that the tree type is a combination of what we called our collection and what we called our tree.

```
IEnumerator Start () {
  m_Tree = BLAgentBehaveLib.InstantiateTree(
      BLAgentBehaveLib.TreeType.NewCollection1_NewTree1, this);
```

```
  while (Application.isPlaying && m_Tree != null) {
    yield return new
    WaitForSeconds(1.0f/m_Tree.Frequency);
    AIUpdate();
  }
}
```

Behave has a real-time loop that calls our own `update` method, `AIUpdate` is the update method we created and is called in a particular interval based on the `frequency` property specified in our tree. Inside our `AIUpdate` method we just called the `Tick` method of our tree instance. [Note: Behave uses the term tick instead of update.]

```
void AIUpdate() {
  m_Tree.Tick();
}
```

There are three methods that we need to implement for our **IAgent** interface. They are as follows:

```
BehaveResult Tick (Tree sender, bool init);
void Reset (Tree sender);
int SelectTopPriority (Tree sender, params int[] IDs);
```

So we'll be implementing them. The `Tick` and `Reset` methods are called whenever an action or a decorator (which we'll discuss later) is, well ticked or reset. If we have implemented our own handler methods for our actions, these methods will be used instead:

```
public BehaveResult Tick(Tree sender, bool init) {
  Debug.Log("Ticked Received by unhandled " +
    (BLAgentBehaveLib.IsAction(sender.ActiveID) ? "Action " :
"Decorator ") +
    " ... " + (BLAgentBehaveLib.IsAction(sender.ActiveID) ?
    ((BLAgentBehaveLib.ActionType)sender.ActiveID).ToString() :
    ((BLAgentBehaveLib.DecoratorType)sender.ActiveID).ToString()));
  return BehaveResult.Success;
}

public void Reset (Tree sender) {

}
```

Inside our generic `Tick` method, we just print out the name of the action or decorator node from the `sender` parameter that receives this tick, as follows:

```
public int SelectTopPriority (Tree sender, params int[] IDs) {
    return 0;
  }
}
```

Again, we'll come back to this `SelectTopPriority` method in a short while. Right now, we'll try to run this behavior. Just create an empty game object and attach this `AgentController` script to it. Then, hit play. If you follow along with this whole section, you should be able to see the nice log messages in the console as shown in the following screenshot:

AngryAnt Behave version 1.4 – Copyright (C) Emil Johansen – AngryAnt 2011
UnityEngine.Debug:Log(Object)

Ticked Received by unhandled Action ... MyAction
UnityEngine.Debug:Log(Object)

Ticked Received by unhandled Action ... MyAction
UnityEngine.Debug:Log(Object)

Unhandled Action results

What that means is now our behavior tree is working together with our script. But as we mentioned before, since we don't have our own handler for the **MyAction** node, the default `Tick` method is called and it's printing this message. So let's go back to our script and write our own handler function for the **MyAction** node, as given in the following code:

```
public BehaveResult TickMyActionAction (Tree sender) {
    Debug.Log ("MyAction ticked!");
    return BehaveResult.Success;
}
```

To implement your own action handler you just need to follow this specific naming pattern, which is `BehaveResult Tick{Name}Action (Tree sender)`. In this example, `{Name}` is the name of our action, **MyAction**. Now if you play the project you'll see the log message printed by your own action handler as follows:

AngryAnt Behave version 1.4 – Copyright (C) Emil Johansen – AngryAnt 2011
UnityEngine.Debug:Log(Object)

MyAction ticked!
UnityEngine.Debug:Log(Object)

MyAction ticked!
UnityEngine.Debug:Log(Object)

Action results

With that you should have a basic understanding of how to use Behave. Next we'll move on to other elements that are used to control the execution flow of actions in our behavior tree.

Decorator

Decorators allow for a conditional entry before executing any node connected to it. Custom handlers for decorators can be implemented in the same way we did for actions previously, but following the naming pattern of `BehaveResult Tick{Name}Decorator (Tree sender)`. If none is defined, the default `Tick` method defined in `IAgent` will be used. So, let's set up our behavior in a new tree or replace the tree we had before with a decorator node as shown in the following screenshot. If you create a new tree, make sure to update the `BLAgentBehaveLib.TreeType` variable in our `Start` function to point to whichever tree you are using. What we want to do is if our new decoration, `ShouldDoMyAction`, returns success, we'll execute the **MyAction** action. Otherwise, we'll not run **MyAction**.

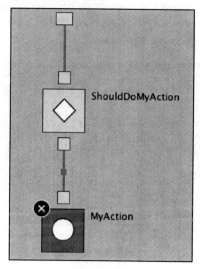

Decorator

The handler method is defined based on the following procedures:

- If `TickDecorator` returns `Success`, the child of the decorator will be ticked and the decorator will return the result of that tick

- If `TickDecorator` returns `Failure`, the child of the decorator will not be ticked and the decorator will return `Success`, which means task completed

- If `TickDecorator` returns `Running`, the child will be ticked and regardless of the result of this tick, the decorator will return `Running`

Now, we'll write our own handler method for the `ShouldDoMyAction` decorator. Please note that the method name must be `TickShouldDoMyActionDecorator` as follows:

```
private bool shouldDo = true;

public BehaveResult TickShouldDoMyActionDecorator (Tree sender) {
  shouldDo = !shouldDo;
  if (shouldDo) {
    Debug.Log ("Should Do!");
    return BehaveResult.Success;
  }
  else {
    Debug.Log ("Shouldn't Do!");
    return BehaveResult.Failure;
  }
}
```

If you run this script, you'll see if the decorator returns `Success` the child node is also called and you'll see the log message printed by the `TickMyActionAction` handler method, as shown in the following screenshot:

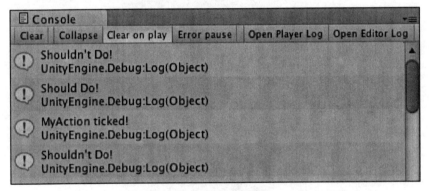

Decorator results

Behave debugger

We can use Behave's built-in debugger to visualize the tree states in live if we build our Behave library for debugging. So let's examine our decorator's state in live using this debugger. First, play the project and navigate to **Window | Behave debugger** to show the debugger window. At the top of the window, you will see a **Tree instances** label. When we play the scene, the name of the currently-loaded tree will appear to the right of this label. Click on the name of the tree to make the tree appear inside the debugger window, as shown in the following screenshot:

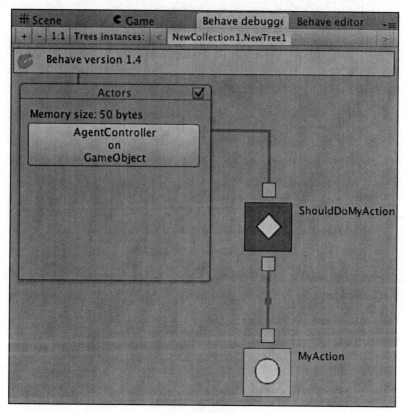

Behave debugger

Sequence

Sequences will tick each of their child nodes connected one at a time from left to right. The actual placement of the nodes is irrelevant. The nodes coming out of the bottom of the sequence determine the order. If a child returns `Failure`, the sequence also returns `Failure` from that point. But if the child returns `Success`, the sequence will move on to the next child inline, and then returns `Running`. Let's set up a tree with a sequence node and connect three actions, **FadeIn**, **FadeOut**, and **GotoGame**.

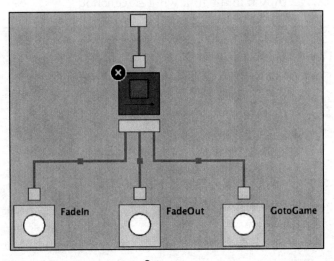

Sequence

Three handler methods for our actions are implemented, and we just simply return `BehaveResult.Success` as follows:

```
public BehaveResult TickFadeInAction (Tree sender) {
  Debug.Log ("FadeIn ticked!");
  return BehaveResult.Success;
}

public BehaveResult TickFadeOutAction (Tree sender) {
  Debug.Log ("FadeOut ticked!");
  return BehaveResult.Success;
}

public BehaveResult TickGotoGameAction (Tree sender) {
  Debug.Log ("GotoGame ticked!");
  return BehaveResult.Success;
}
```

If we run the project now, you'll see the three actions discussed previously are getting called sequentially.

If a child returns Running, the sequence will also return Running from that point and that same child will be ticked again the next time the sequence is ticked.

Once the sequence reaches the end of its child list, it returns Success and the first child in the line will be ticked on the next tick of the sequence.

Exploring Behave results

Now let's update our handler methods to play with other Behave results. We'll increase the alpha value during the FadeIn action, and until it reaches 255, we'll return Running from the FadeIn action as given in the following code:

```
private int alpha = 0;
private int gameLoading = 0;

public BehaveResult TickFadeInAction (Tree sender) {
  if (gameLoading >= 100) {
    return BehaveResult.Failure;
  }

  alpha++;
  Debug.Log ("FadeIn ticked! Alpha:" + alpha.ToString());
  if (alpha < 255) {
    return BehaveResult.Running;
  }
  else {
    alpha = 255;
    return BehaveResult.Success;
  }
}
```

So, the sequence will not move on to next child and will keep ticking this FadeIn action. Only when the alpha reaches to 255, this action will return Success and the sequence will move on to the next child node. Once we have reached the GotoGame action and until the gameLoading progress has reached 100 we'll only return Failure so that will not start this sequence again until the loading is complete.

The next action is the `FadeOut` action and it'll decrease the `alpha` value. Similar to `FadeIn`, until it reaches 0, we'll only return `Running`. So, the sequence will also return `Running` and when the sequence is ticked the next time, it'll tick starting from this action. This is something to note with the `Running` result that it'll resume from that child node and not from the left-most child.

```
public BehaveResult TickFadeOutAction (Tree sender) {
    alpha--;
    Debug.Log ("FadeOut ticked! Alpha:" + alpha.ToString());
    if (alpha > 0) {
        return BehaveResult.Running;
    }
    else {
        alpha = 0;
        return BehaveResult.Success;
    }
}
```

Finally when the `FadeOut` action returns `Success`, the sequence will move on to the `GotoGame` action and increase the `gameLoading` value. Once this value reaches 100, we'll return `Success`, otherwise, we'll only return `Running`, as given in the following code:

```
public BehaveResult TickGotoGameAction (Tree sender) {
    gameLoading++;
    Debug.Log ("GotoGame ticked! Game loading: " +
        gameLoading.ToString());
    if (gameLoading < 100) {
        return BehaveResult.Running;
    }
    else {
        return BehaveResult.Success;
    }
}
```

We just used all three Behave results, `Success`, `Failure`, and `Running` in the preceding example. Before we test this, we need to temporary increase the `Frequency` value (for example, 25). Otherwise it will take it 10 minutes for our sequence to complete! Now, let's move on to other behavior tree elements.

Selector

Selectors are like a nested `if` statements and tick each of their children once at a time from left to right. If a child returns `Success`, the selector also returns `Success` from that point. But if a child returns `Failure`, the selector will move on to the next child in line and return `Running`. If a child returns `Running`, so does the selector and that same child will be ticked again the next time the selector is ticked. Once the selector reaches the end of its child list, it returns `Failure` and starts ticking from the first child again on the next tick of the selector.

In this exercise, we'll set up a tree as shown in the following screenshot; a selector and three actions: **Patrol**, **Attack**, and **Idle**.

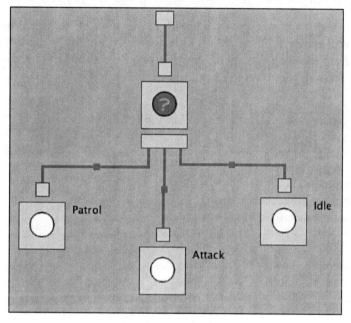

Selector

In our `patrol` action we'll decrease the distance with the `enemy` variable and check if it's close enough to this agent. If it's not close enough we'll just return `Running` and the selector will also return `Running` from this point, as follows:

```
private int distWithEnemy = 200;
private int enemyHealth = 100;

public BehaveResult TickPatrolAction (Tree sender) {
    if (distWithEnemy > 100) {
        distWithEnemy-=10;
```

```
        Debug.Log("Enemy is getting closers! " + distWithEnemy.
ToString());
        return BehaveResult.Running;
    }
    else {
      Debug.Log("Enemy spotted!");
      return BehaveResult.Failure;
    }
  }
```

Once the `distance` variable is less than `100` we'll return `Failure`, meaning that the enemy is close enough and we shouldn't stick at `patrol` action anymore. And our selector will move on to next child node, which is the `attack` action in our case.

We attack our enemy and decrease it's health in our `attack` action. While during the attack we will return `Running`. And only when the enemy is dead we return `Failure`, meaning that our enemy is now dead and we shouldn't attack anymore. Then, the selector will move on to next child node, which is the `idle` action, as follows:

```
public BehaveResult TickAttackAction (Tree sender) {
    enemyHealth-=5;
    Debug.Log("Attacking enemy! enemy health: " + enemyHealth.ToString
());
    if (enemyHealth < 10) {
      Debug.Log("Enemy's dead!");
      return BehaveResult.Failure;
    }
    else {
      return BehaveResult.Running;
    }
  }


public BehaveResult TickIdleAction (Tree sender) {
    distWithEnemy = 200;
    enemyHealth = 100;
    Debug.Log("Idling for a while!");
    return BehaveResult.Success;
  }
```

So if you run this behavior tree you should see a list of log messages in your console that looks something like the following screenshot. Our AI agent is now patrolling, checking the distance with enemy, attacking accordingly to our behavior tree and script:

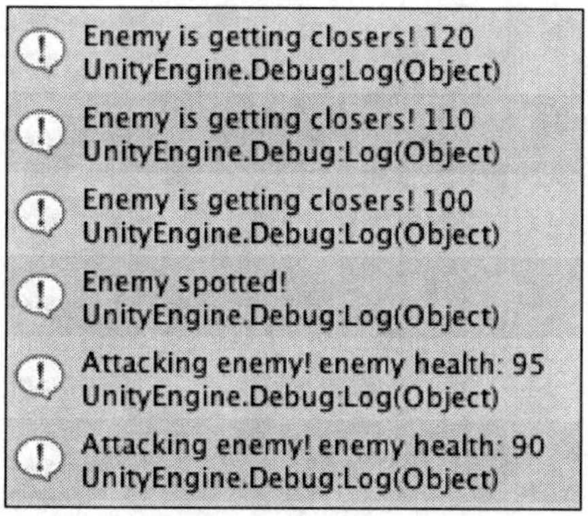

The battle between robots and aliens

Priority selector

When ticked, a priority selector will query the agent through its `SelectTopPriority` method for the highest priority of its outgoing connections. The priority selector will then tick the connection corresponding to the returned index ID and its return value is passed on. If the ticked connection returns `Running`, then the priority selector will not requery priority on next tick. If a priority query returns the `Unknown` priority ID or an ID outside the queried set, the priority selector will return `Failure`.

So let's create a tree as shown in the following figure with a priority selector and three actions, **Eat**, **Sleep**, and **Play**.

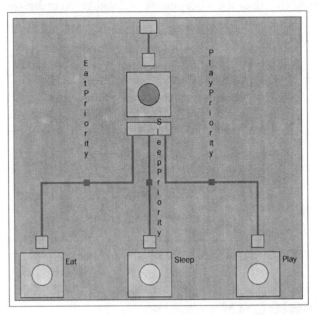

Priority Selector

It's important to note that the orders of output connections are important, as their index values will be used to reference from the script. So, in this sample connection index, the eat action would be 0, sleep would be 1, and play would be 2. And our `SelectTopPrioirty` method is implemented as follows:

```
private bool isHungry = true;
private bool isSleepy = true;

public int SelectTopPriority (Tree sender, params int[] IDs) {
  if (isHungry) {
    isHungry = false;
    isSleepy = true;
    return IDs[0]; //eat
  }
  else if (isSleepy) {
    isSleepy = false;
    return IDs[1]; //sleep
  }
  else {
    isHungry = true;
    return IDs[2]; //play
  }
}
```

We give priority to the eat action if isHungry is true and the sleep action if isSleepy is true. Otherwise we choose the play action. Unlike sequences and selectors, priority selectors don't need to go through in order, and instead we can straight away return a relevant action based on the conditions.

What if you need multiple priority selectors in one tree?

A quick Internet search leads to an answer from *AngryAnt* on Github's Bahave issues list that suggests to use a selector's context variable to identify which selector is being called in the SelectTopPriority method.

You can find this and other solutions at https://github.com/AngryAnt/Behave-release/issues/.

Parallel

The parallel node ticks all of its children each time it is ticked from left to right. There are two important settings for the parallel node called child completion and component completion. The child completion parameter determines how the child's return values are handled as follows:

- If set to SuccessOrFailure, a child output is marked as done whenever that child returns success or failure

- If set to Success, that child will only get the done stamp if it returns Success. A return of Failure will result in the parallel component returning Failure after having ticked all the children

- The Failure setting works in the same way. The child will only get the done stamp if it returns Failure

The component completion parameter determines when the parallel node returns Success based on the child node's done stamp as follows:

- If set to One, the parallel component will return Success at the end of the first tick where one child's output has been marked as done

- If it is set to All, the parallel component will continue running until all children have been marked as done

- Until the parallel node can return either Success or Failure, each tick on it will result in Running

It'd be easier to understand if we look through an example. So, let's set up a tree with a sequence node at the root, a parallel node with two actions, and another action connected to the sequence node. It should look something like the following screenshot:

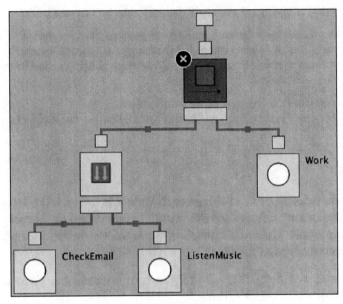

Parallel node

We'll set the `Component completion` variable on the parallel node to `All` and the `Child completion` variable to `Success`. So, that means if all the actions, `CheckEmail` and `ListenMusic`, return `Success`, they'll be marked as done and the parallel node will return `Success`. Otherwise, it'll return `Failure`, and thus the parent sequence node will also return `Failure` from that point, resulting in the work action, which never gets called.

So, let's implement the action handlers for `CheckEmail` and `ListenMusic`. We'll return `Failure` from the `ListenMusic` action as given in the following code and see what happens:

```
public BehaveResult TickCheckEmailAction (Tree sender) {
  Debug.Log("Checking email");
  return BehaveResult.Success;
}

public BehaveResult TickListenMusicAction (Tree sender) {
  Debug.Log("While listening music!");
  return BehaveResult.Failure;
}
```

You'll notice that the work action was never called. Then change the `ListenMusic` action code to return `Success`. Now all the actions under the parallel node return `Success`, so it'll also return `Success` and the sequence will continue to the work action.

Reference

When you create another behavior tree in your collection, that tree will be available in other trees as a reference. When references are ticked, the tree set in the parameter of the `reference` will be ticked and the `reference` will return the result of that tree. References are a nice way to organize various different behavior trees in your project.

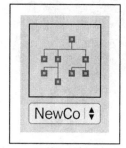

Reference node

The Robots versus Aliens project

This chapter comes with a sample project called Robots versus Aliens that demonstrates the use of Behave behavior trees in a real-game prototype. Open the project in Unity3D and we'll walk through briefly. The game demo and the agents' AI are pretty simple. This is how the scene is set up, as shown in the following screenshot:

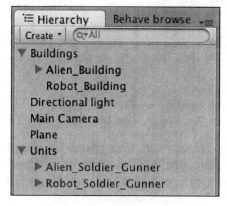

Scene hierarchy

There are two AI agents in this game, robot and alien. At the start of the game, units from each side will be spawned and each of them will march toward the enemy's base. The Alien base looks similar to the following screenshot:

Alien base

And the Robot base looks similar to the following screenshot:

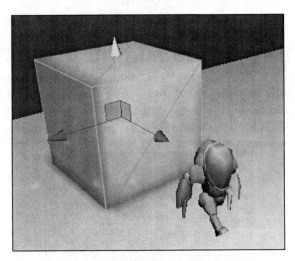

Robot base

Once they are at a certain distance they'll start attacking, and once the other side has died it'll move forward again until they reach the base. Once they reach the base, they'll just attack the base. Click on **AgentBehaveLibrary** in the project panel and click on **Edit Library** from the property inspector. We have one collection and one tree called **AgentAI**, as shown in the following screenshot:

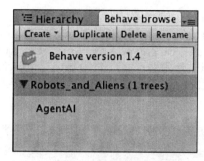

Behave browser

This is how their AI behavior tree is structured, as shown in the following screenshot:

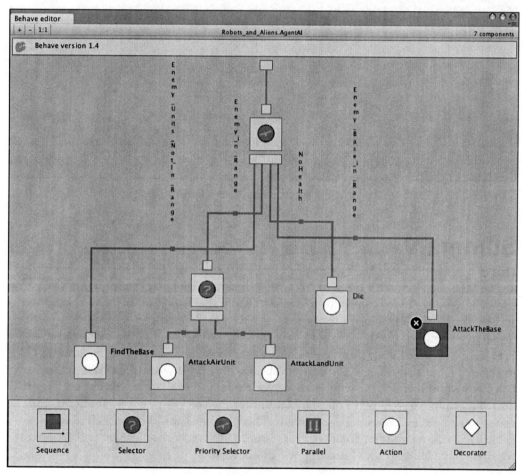

Robot versus Alien behavior tree

There are three main scripts in this project, `AlienController` for the alien AI, `RobotController` for the robot AI and the base `AgentAI` class, which is inherited by both of the controller classes. You can run through the project and check the action states using the Behave debugger. We'll not list and go through all the code here since all the scripts are well commented on, and you should be able to understand it by reading it yourself.

Robots versus Aliens

Summary

This chapter introduces behavior trees in general and uses the Behave system to implement such behavior trees in Unity3D. There are six basic components you can use in Behave behavior tree; action, decorator, parallel, selector, priority selector, and sequence. Each has its own purpose and we briefly covered each of them with respective samples. Lastly here are a few things to remember while using Behave. You have to rebuild your library whenever you make changes to the trees so that the changes are also reflected in compiled code library. If your tree is not getting any ticks, you should check the frequency of your tree and make sure it's not set to zero. You need to make sure that you're instantiating the correct tree type that you want to use in your `InstantiateTree` statement. This chapter should be sufficient for you to get started using behavior trees in your game. In the next chapter, we will pull from what we have learned into building one final project.

10
Putting It All Together

Over the previous nine chapters, we looked at various AI techniques and built some simple demo applications using Unity3D. This is the final chapter in our book and we'll apply some of those techniques in a better game example. The techniques we'll be using in this chapter include pathfinding, finite-state machines (FSMs) and flocking behavior together with some other generic game features, such as building classes for weapons and ammos. So unlike the other chapters this one should be a bit more fun. First we will create the car. Then we will give it some AI. After that we will outfit our cars with weapons for battle. Let's get started.

In this chapter, we'll be building a simple vehicular combat game inspired by the popular *Twisted Metal* series on the PlayStation platform. So, of course, there'll be cars and gunfights and explosions, but it will be much simpler in our version. This project after all is still a demo, and we will not be building a complete game with scoring systems, power ups, menu screens, and customization stuff. So in a scaled down version of our vehicular combat game, we'll implement a player-controlled car and an AI class for opponent cars. The player car will be equipped with two different weapons; a normal gun with bullets and a missile launcher that will track down if targeted at an enemy car.

Scene setup

So let's get started with how our scene has been structured.

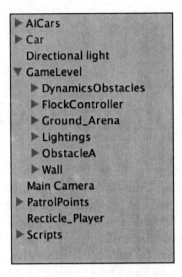

The objects in the hierarchy

We have four AI cars grouped under the **AICars** entity and one player-controlled car entity.

The realistic car model, car movement behaviors and camera scripts were based on the Unity3D Car Tutorial project. You can download and learn more about it at `http://u3d.as/content/unity-technologies/car-tutorial/`.

We have also set up waypoints for AI cars to patrol and a flock controller group with the objects as child entities under it. If you want to build a more realistic environment you could add other types of light, and build a light map to generate shadows for an offline mode. But in this demo, we'll just use a directional light to simply light up the scene. The `recticle` player game object is used to reference the target position pointed by the mouse. In addition to static block obstacles we also have dynamic obstacles that are affected by physics and can be destroyed by our weapons. So this is what our little scene looks like:

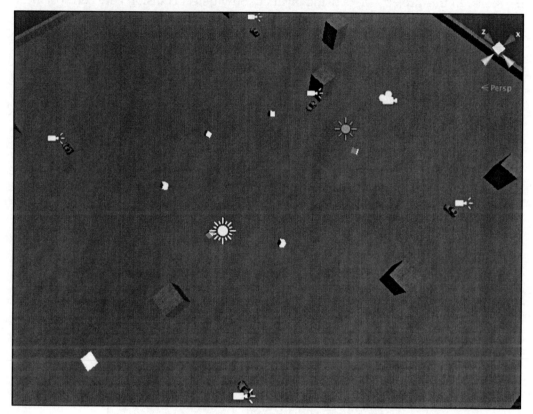

How the scene looks from above

Tags and layers

Before we start scripting there's one important step to set up, which is to configure tags used in our game. Tags and layers can be set up through **Edit | Project Settings | Tags**. We can use either object names or tags when referencing and identifying game objects in the scene from a script using methods like `GameObject.FindWithTag()`. Layers are mostly used while setting a culling mask for cameras to render only the selected parts of the scene, and by lights to illuminate only parts of the scene. In this project, we're using layers to only detect collision between specific layers. We'll see more on that later, when we use them in scripting. For now, just take note that tags and layers are set up as shown in the following screenshot:

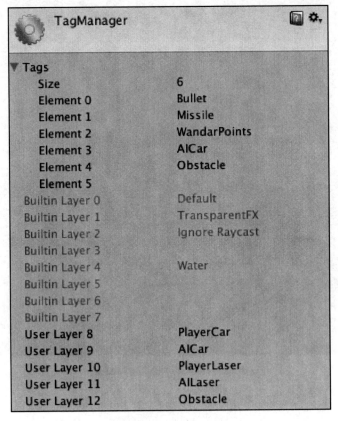

Tags and layers used in our game

Vehicles

As mentioned earlier the car model and behavior scripts are based on the Unity3D car tutorial. Some of the scripts written in JavaScript were converted to C# just to make them consistent.

Our car outfitted with weapons

We added three additional components to our base car model. They are missile launchers on each side of the car body and a normal gun model with a rotatable turret on the top. Also, take note that the player car uses the **Player** tag and enemy cars use the **AICar** tag that we defined earlier.

Modifications added to our car

Player car controller

Player car has a few different scripts attached to it. Basically `Car.cs` and `PlayerCarController.cs` take care of the car movement in a realistic way. Since realistic car physics is a huge subject, and as you can also learn from the Unity3D car tutorial, we'll be looking more into our project specific scripts and controllers in this chapter. The following is our `PlayerWeaponController` class that controls the aiming and shooting of our two different weapons:

```
using UnityEngine;
using System.Collections;

public class PlayerWeaponController : MonoBehaviour{
  public WeaponGun gun;
  public WeaponMissile[] missile; //Left and Right missile pod
  public Transform Turret;

  //The Recticle object, the mouse cursor graphic
  private Transform recticle;

  // Use this for initialization
  void Start () {
    if (!recticle)
      recticle = GameObject.Find("Recticle_Player").transform;
  }

  // Update is called once per frame
  void Update () {
    //Shoot laser from the turret
    if (Input.GetMouseButtonDown(0)) {
      gun.Shoot();
    }
    else if (Input.GetMouseButtonUp(0)) {
      gun.StopShoot();
    }

    //Shoot missile from the turret
    if (Input.GetMouseButtonDown(1)) {
      missile[1].Shoot();
    }
    else if (Input.GetMouseButtonUp(1)) {
      missile[1].StopShoot();
    }
```

```
//Rotate the turret
//AIMING WITH THE MOUSE
//Generate a plane that intersects the transform's
    //position with an upwards normal.
Plane playerPlane = new Plane(Vector3.up, transform.position);

// Generate a ray from the cursor position
Ray RayCast =
    Camera.main.ScreenPointToRay(Input.mousePosition);

// Determine the point where the cursor ray intersects the
    //plane.
float HitDist = 0;

if (playerPlane.Raycast(RayCast, out HitDist)) {
  // Get the point along the ray that hits the calculated
    //distance.
  Vector3 targetPoint = RayCast.GetPoint(HitDist);

  //Set the position of the Recticle to be the same as the
  //position of the mouse on the created plane

  recticle.position = targetPoint;
  Turret.LookAt(recticle.position);
    }
  }
}
```

We begin with taking reference entities for missile weapons and the rotatable turret. We have yet to create the WeaponGun class or the WeaponMissile class, but we will, later on in the chapter. The recticle is a separate empty game object in our scene. In the start method, we try to find that object in the scene, and store a reference in our local recticle. Then in our Update method, we use the left mouse button click event to trigger normal bullet shooting and the right mouse button to shoot missiles. We then pick the current position of the mouse pointer in 2D space and convert it into 3D space by raycasting. This has been explained in *Chapter 2, Finite State Machines*, in the section titled *Controlling the tank*. Then the turret object attached to the car is rotated to look at that direction, and also the recticle position is updated. This position of the recticle image is updated in real-time as well.

AI Car Controller

We will apply the `AdvancedFSM` framework that we built in *Chapter 2, Finite State Machines*, to implement the enemy car's AI. The `AICarController` class is extended from the `AdvancedFSM` class and set ups the FSM framework.

```
using UnityEngine;
using System.Collections;

public class AICarController : AdvancedFSM {
  protected override void Initialise() {
    //Start Doing the Finite State Machine
    ConstructFSM();

    //Get the target enemy(Player)
    GameObject objPlayer =
        GameObject.FindGameObjectWithTag("Player");
    playerTransform = objPlayer.transform;

    if (!playerTransform)
      print("Player doesn't exist.. Please add one with " +
          "Tag named 'Player'");
  }
```

We have to make sure that there's a player object with the tag `Player` in the scene. If found, we'll store this object reference in the `playerTransform` variable. Then we set up our transitions and states in the `ConstructFSM` method.

```
  //Construct the Finite State Machine for the AI Car behavior
  private void ConstructFSM() {
    //Get the list of points
    pointList = GameObject.FindGameObjectsWithTag("WandarPoints");
    Transform[] waypoints = new Transform[pointList.Length];
    int i = 0;
    foreach (GameObject obj in pointList) {
      waypoints[i] = obj.transform;
      i++;
    }

    PatrolState patrol = new PatrolState(waypoints);
    patrol.AddTransition(Transition.SawPlayer,
        FSMStateID.Chasing);
    patrol.AddTransition(Transition.NoHealth, FSMStateID.Dead);
```

```
ChaseState chase = new ChaseState(waypoints);
chase.AddTransition(Transition.LostPlayer,
    FSMStateID.Patrolling);
chase.AddTransition(Transition.ReachPlayer,
    FSMStateID.Attacking);
chase.AddTransition(Transition.NoHealth, FSMStateID.Dead);

AttackState attack = new AttackState(waypoints);
attack.AddTransition(Transition.LostPlayer,
    FSMStateID.Patrolling);
attack.AddTransition(Transition.SawPlayer,
    FSMStateID.Chasing);
attack.AddTransition(Transition.NoHealth, FSMStateID.Dead);

DeadState dead = new DeadState();
dead.AddTransition(Transition.NoHealth, FSMStateID.Dead);

AddFSMState(patrol);
AddFSMState(chase);
AddFSMState(attack);
AddFSMState(dead);
}
```

We set up a couple of points in our scene to use as waypoints for our AI cars to navigate in the scene.

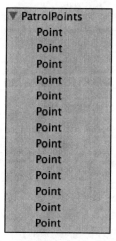

Our scene needs a lot of points

These waypoints use the tag **WandarPoints**. So the first thing we have to do, while constructing our FSM, is to find all those points tagged as **WandarPoints** and pass them to our AI states so that they are aware of their environment.

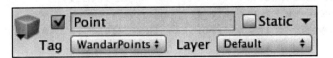

Patrol Points tagged as WandarPoints

After that, we create states and transition triggers and adding into our FSM framework.

Finite State Machines (FSMs)

We need to set up an update loop that will call the `Reason` and `Act` methods from our various `State` classes. We'll look at the implementation of these states in a while.

```
protected override void CarFixedUpdate() {
    CurrentState.Reason(playerTransform, transform);
    CurrentState.Act(playerTransform, transform);
}
```

Since we separate the different states of our AI car into different classes, our `update` method is much simpler. We only need to call the reason and act methods of the current state of the AI. To represent the FSM model of our AI cars in a state transition diagram, it would look something like this.

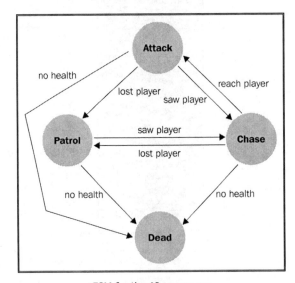

FSM for the AI enemy car

And the last part is taking damage based on collision with either bullets or missiles. Once the health reaches less than or equal to zero, we'll play a nice physics-based explosion effect, destroy the object, and finally remove it from the scene.

```
//Hit with Missile or Bullet
void OnCollisionEnter(Collision collision) {
  if (bDead)
    return;

  if (collision.gameObject.tag == "Bullet") {
    print("AICar Hit with Bullet");
    health -= 30;
  }
  else if (collision.gameObject.tag == "Missile") {
    print("AICar Hit with Missile");
    health -= 50;
  }

  if (health <= 0) {
    bDead = true;
    Explode();
    Destroy(gameObject, 4.0f);
  }
}
```

Patrol state

Each state in our FSM has two main methods, Reason and Act. Basically, the Reason method checks the condition, and takes care of transition to other states. In our patrol state, the Reason method checks the distance between the player and current AI car position. If it's close enough, it'll set the transition to SawPlayer. We've already set up mapping between transitions and states for each of our AI car objects.

```
public override void Reason(Transform player, Transform npc) {
  if (Vector3.Distance(npc.position, player.position) <= 100.0f) {
    Debug.Log("Switch to Chase State");
    npc.GetComponent<AICarController>().SetTransition(
        Transition.SawPlayer);
    npc.GetComponent<AICarController>().throttle = 0.0f;
    npc.GetComponent<AICarController>().DoHandbrake();
  }
}
```

So, later in our `AdvancedFSM` class, this new transition is used to retrieve the current state correctly. The following is the `PerformTransition` method of the `AdvancedFSM` class that handles this state transition.

```
public void PerformTransition(Transition trans) {
  // Check if the currentState has the transition passed as
    //argument
  FSMStateID id = currentState.GetOutputState(trans);
  if (id == FSMStateID.None) {
    Debug.LogError("FSM ERROR: Current State does not have a " +
        "target state for this transition");
    return;
  }

  // Update the currentStateID and currentState
  currentStateID = id;
  foreach (FSMState state in fsmStates) {
    if (state.ID == currentStateID) {
      currentState = state;
      break;
    }
  }
}
```

And the `Act` method of our Patrol states will find the next waypoint, if the AI car is already near the current destination point, and will update the direction and speed accordingly.

```
public override void Act(Transform player, Transform npc) {
  //Find another random patrol point if the current point is
  //reached
  if (Vector3.Distance(npc.position, destPos) <= 5.0f) {
    FindNextPoint();
    curPathIndex = 0;
    //Brake it first before moving to the next point
    npc.GetComponent<AICarController>().DoHandbrake();
  }
}
```

Chase state

The `Reason` method checks and transitions to `ReachPlayer`, if the distance between the player and the AI car is close enough. Otherwise, it'll update the transition to `LostPlayer`. So the `ReachPlayer` transition will update the AI state to the `Attack` state while `LostPlayer` will make the AI car go back to `Patrol` state.

```
//Check the new reason to change state
public override void Reason(Transform player, Transform npc) {
    //Set the target position as the player position
    destPos = player.position;

    //Check the distance with player tank
    //When the distance is near, transition to attack state
    float dist = Vector3.Distance(npc.position, destPos);
    if (dist <= 60.0f) {
        Debug.Log("Switch to Attack state");
        npc.GetComponent<AICarController>().SetTransition(
            Transition.ReachPlayer);
    }

    //Go back to patrol is it become too far
    if (dist >= 110.0f) {
    Debug.Log("Switch to Patrol state");
    npc.GetComponent<AICarController>().SetTransition(
        Transition.LostPlayer);
    }
}
```

The Chase state's `Act` method is short but requires some background on linear algebra and trigonometry.

```
//Action taken in the current state
public override void Act(Transform player, Transform npc) {
    //Rotate to the target point
    destPos = player.position;

    npc.GetComponent<AICarController>().throttle = 1.0f;

    Vector3 RelativeWaypointPosition =
        npc.InverseTransformPoint(new Vector3(destPos.x,
            npc.position.y, destPos.z));

    npc.GetComponent<AICarController>().steer =
        RelativeWaypointPosition.x /
        RelativeWaypointPosition.magnitude;
}
```

Unity3D has a method called `InverseTransformPoint` that translates a position from world space to local space. Currently the player position is in world space. So, we use this method to find the relative position of the target player car position from the AI car transform. `RelativeWaypointPosition` holds the new vector (x, y, z), which is also the direction vector to the player car from the AI car.

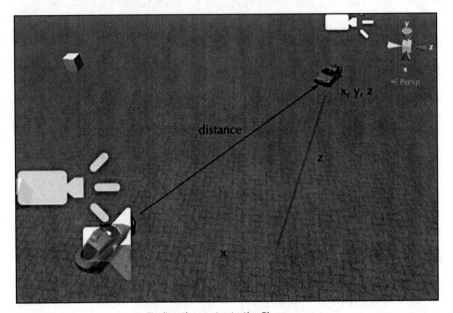

Finding the vector to the Player car

Once we get this vector we can determine by what degree we need to rotate, if any, towards the direction of player car by dividing the horizontal position by the vector magnitude or distance. We then apply this angular value to steer the wheels toward the player car.

Attack state

When the player is close enough to the AI car, we can reach the `Attack state`. We'll rotate the gun towards the player car and start shooting coroutine.

```
public override void Act(Transform player, Transform npc) {
    //Set the target position as the player position
    destPos = player.position + new Vector3(0.0f, 1.0f, 0.0f);

    Transform turret = weapon.Turret;
    Quaternion turretRotation = Quaternion.LookRotation(
        destPos - turret.position);
```

```
turret.rotation = Quaternion.Slerp(turret.rotation,
    turretRotation, Time.deltaTime * curRotSpeed);

//Shoot shouldn't call every frame
if (!bStartShooting) {
  //Shoot bullet/Missiles towards the player
  ShootShells();
  bStartShooting = true;
}
}
```

In our `Reason` method, we check the distance with the player and set the transition back to either `LostPlayer` or `SawPlayer`. These transitions will update the current state to patrol state or chase state.

```
public override void Reason(Transform player, Transform npc) {
  //Check the distance with the player car
  float dist = Vector3.Distance(npc.position,player.position);
  if (dist >= 50.0f && dist < 100.0f) {
    Debug.Log("Switch to Chase State");
    npc.GetComponent<AICarController>().SetTransition(
        Transition.SawPlayer);
    StopShooting();
  }

  //Transition to patrol is the tank become too far
  else if (dist >= 100.0f) {
    Debug.Log("Switch to Patrol State");
    npc.GetComponent<AICarController>().SetTransition(
        Transition.LostPlayer);
    StopShooting();
  }
}
```

Weapons

Our player-controlled car has two weapons; a missile launcher and a normal gun, while the AI cars only have a normal gun. Let us look at them to see how they're implemented. There are not many AI techniques here though.

Gun

The WeaponGun class simply spawns bullets upon calling its Shoot method.

```
using UnityEngine;
using System.Collections;

public class WeaponGun : MonoBehaviour {
  public GameObject Bullet;
  public GameObject[] GunGraphics;
  public float ratePerSecond;
  private bool bShoot;

  // Use this for initialization
  void Start() {
    bShoot = false;
  }

  public void Shoot() {
    bShoot = true;

    foreach (GameObject obj in GunGraphics) {
      obj.animation.CrossFade("GunShooting", 0.5f);
    }

    StartCoroutine("ShootBullets");
  }
```

When shooting bullets we don't want to instantiate too many bullets at once because of a high frames per second rating. Instead, we would like to limit the shooting rate to a specific user defined value. We want to wait for a specific duration before spawning another bullet. We can do this by using coroutines in Unity3D.

```
  public void StopShoot() {
    //Stop the shooting animation
    if (bShoot) {
      bShoot = false;

      foreach (GameObject obj in GunGraphics) {
        obj.animation.Stop("GunShooting");
      }
    }

    StopCoroutine("ShootBullets");
  }
```

As explained in the Unity3D reference, a `coroutine` is a function that can suspend its execution (yield), until the given `YieldInstruction` finishes. We can start and stop coroutines using the `StartCoroutine` and `StopCoroutine` methods. The following is our `coroutine` method, `ShootBullets`. In this method, we wait for a certain number of milliseconds based on the specified `ratePerSecond` value.

```
private IEnumerator ShootBullets() {
    SpawnBullet();
    yield return new WaitForSeconds(1.0f / ratePerSecond);
    StartCoroutine("ShootBullets");
}
```

This `coroutine` method just calls our `SpawnBullet` method that instantiates a new Bullet prefab at a random position and rotation along the gun's position.

```
private void SpawnBullet() {
    int rndSpawnPoint = Random.Range(0, GunGraphics.Length);
    Vector3 SpawnPos =
        GunGraphics[rndSpawnPoint].transform.position;
    Quaternion SpawnRot =
        GunGraphics[rndSpawnPoint].transform.rotation;

    //Create a new Bullet
    GameObject objBullet = (GameObject)Instantiate(Bullet,
        SpawnPos, SpawnRot);
    }
}
```

Bullet

The `Bullet` object is set up as a prefab called `PlayerLaser`. In the chapter assets, you can find it under **Assets | Resources | Prefabs | Bullets**.

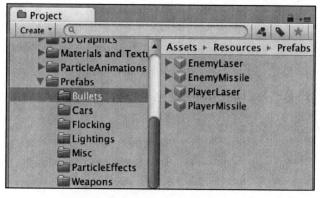

Location of all our weapons

The `Bullet` behavior class is added to this laser bullet prefab. It also has a rigid body and box collider components, so that we can detect collision with other objects. We also need a particle effect to be played when it hits something.

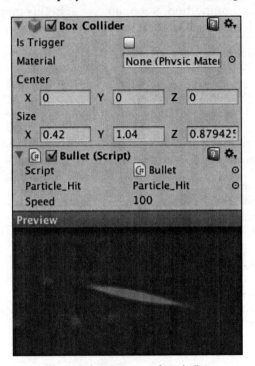

Setup and appearance of our bullet

And here's our `Bullet` class. The first thing we do in our `Start` method is to destroy this bullet game object automatically after two seconds.

```
using UnityEngine;
using System.Collections;

public class Bullet : MonoBehaviour {
  public GameObject Particle_Hit;
  public float speed = 100.0f;

  // Use this for initialization
  void Start() {
    Destroy(gameObject, 2.0f);
  }
```

And in the `update` method, we just move advance in the positive Z direction to move forward with a defined speed.

```
// Update is called once per frame
void Update () {
  transform.Translate(new Vector3(0, 0, speed *
      Time.deltaTime));
}

void OnCollisionEnter(Collision collision) {
  Vector3 contactPoint = collision.contacts[0].point;

  Instantiate(Particle_Hit, contactPoint, Quaternion.identity);
  Destroy(gameObject);
  }
}
```

The `OnCollisionEnter` method is called when this game object collides with something. We just play the bullet particle effect attached and destroy the bullet object. The other game object being hit by the bullet will handle the damaging taking and state switching tasks.

Launcher

The missile launcher weapon is also similar to the gun weapon class. It spawns missiles, and uses coroutines to wait for a few milliseconds between each missile instantiation. The only difference with the gun weapon is missiles have a mode to lock and chase down the target if the player aims and shoots correctly on an enemy AI car.

```
using UnityEngine;
using System.Collections;

public class WeaponMissile: MonoBehaviour {
  public GameObject Missile;
  public Transform SpawnPoint;
  private bool bShoot, bHasTarget;
  private Transform target;

  // Use this for initialization
  void Start() {
    bShoot = false;
    bHasTarget = false;
  }
```

Then, we initialize our properties in the `Start` method. And in the `Shoot` method we use raycasting to test if there's an AI car at the current mouse position.

```
public void Shoot() {
  //Check Whether target exist or not
  Ray ray = Camera.main.ScreenPointToRay(Input.mousePosition);
  RaycastHit hitInfo;

  //RayCast only to AI Car which layer number is 9
    int layerMask = 1 << 9;

  if (Physics.Raycast(ray, out hitInfo, 1000.0f, layerMask)) {
    bHasTarget = true;
    target = hitInfo.transform;
  }
  else {
    bHasTarget = false;
  }

  bShoot = true;
  StartCoroutine("ShootMissiles");
}
```

The `Raycast` method's layer mask parameter determines which layers to test against with the ray generated. AI car layer we set up at layer number 9 previously. By bit shifting the number one, (...0000000001) in binary, nine places to the left, becomes (...001000000000) in binary. The result is that all the layers except layer 9 will be neglected while performing raycasting. If that ray hits with an AI car, then we'll set `bHasTarget` to `true` and set the target transformation. Afterwards, we start the `ShootMissiles` coroutine.

```
public void StopShoot() {
  //Stop the shooting animation
  if (bShoot) {
    bShoot = false;
  }
  StopCoroutine("ShootMissiles");
}

private IEnumerator ShootMissiles() {
  SpawnMissile();
  yield return new WaitForSeconds(
      Random.Range(0.3f, 0.6f));
  StartCoroutine("ShootMissiles");
}
```

```
   private void SpawnMissile() {
      //Create a new Missile
       GameObject objMissile = (GameObject)Instantiate(Missile,
         SpawnPoint.position, SpawnPoint.rotation);

      objMissile.GetComponent<Missile>().Initialise(bHasTarget,
         target);
   }
}
```

Finally, in the `SpawnMissile` method, we instantiate a new missile prefab at the missile weapon position. Then, we get the `Missile` script, and tell it if we have a target and what that target is.

Missile

Our `WeaponMissile` or `launcher` weapon class spawns each missile. During initialization we check whether there is a target object to chase and destroy for this missile.

```
using UnityEngine;
using System.Collections;

public class Missile : MonoBehaviour {
   public GameObject Particle_Hit;
   public float speed = 20.0f;
   private Transform target;

   public void Initialise(bool bHasTarget, Transform target
      = null) {
     if (bHasTarget) {
       this.target = target;
       Destroy(gameObject, 4.0f);
     }
     else {
       Destroy(gameObject, 2.0f);
     }
   }
```

If there's a target object then in our `Update` method, we constantly track the target position and update the direction and rotation values of our missile accordingly.

```
// Update is called once per frame
void Update() {
  if (target != null) {
    //Make the target position upwards alittle bit
    Vector3 newTarPos = target.position +
        new Vector3(0.0f, 1.0f, 0.0f);

    //Rotate towards the target
    Vector3 tarDir = newTarPos - transform.position;
    Quaternion tarRot = Quaternion.LookRotation(tarDir);
    transform.rotation=Quaternion.Slerp(transform.rotation,
        tarRot, 3.0f * Time.deltaTime);
  }

  transform.Translate(new Vector3(0, 0,
      speed * Time.deltaTime));
}
```

Finally, like in our `bullet` class, when the missile hits something we just play the explosion particle effect and destroy the `missile` object.

```
void OnCollisionEnter(Collision collision) {
  Vector3 contactPoint = collision.contacts[0].point;

  Instantiate(Particle_Hit, contactPoint,
      Quaternion.identity);
  Destroy(gameObject);
  }
}
```

This will produce a cool effect of the target locked missile launched from the side of the car, as shown in the following screenshot:

Firing missiles at our enemies

Summary

In this chapter, we applied some of the AI techniques that we learned previously to our simple vehicular combat game. We would be able to apply some more techniques in a larger game scope, but in this short chapter, we reused the advanced FSM framework that we built in *Chapter 2, Finite State Machines*, as well as waypoint and path following techniques. We could also use our sensor system, while detecting the environment for the AI cars. But to make the chapter simpler we just accessed the player's position and checked the distance between the two directly. The AI cars will follow and attack once the player car is near them, even if it's not in their line of sight. So this is one area you can apply in order to make the game better. This is the final chapter of this book, and we hope that you learnt something new in areas related to artificial intelligence in games as well as in Unity3D.

Index

A

A* algorithm
  about 123, 124
  testing 141, 142
action 164, 165
AdvancedFSM class 196
AdvancedFSM framework 192
AdvanceFSM class 53 48, 49
Agent 115
AgentAI class 184
AgentController.cs file 166
AI
  about 5
  in games 6
  research areas 6
  sensory systems 76
  techniques 7
AI car controller 192, 194
AICars entity 186
AI character
  about 81, 82
  perspective sense 83-85
  sense class 83
  testing 88
  touch sense 86, 87
AIUpdate method 167
Aliens project
  versus Robots project 181-184
alignment rule 11
A* pathfinding algorithm 13-20
ArrayList type 126
Artificial Intelligence. *See* **AI**
Aspect.cs class 81
Aspect.cs file 81
aspectName 81

AssignNeighbour method 131
AStar class 123 132-134
AStar.FindPath method 136
attack state 44, 198
avoidanceForce property 92
avoidanceRadius property 92
AvoidObstacles method 117-119

B

behave plugin
  about 160
  debugger 171
  downloading, steps for 160, 161
  installing, steps for 160, 161
  results, exploring 173, 174
Behave.Runtime namespace 166
behavior trees 23-25
betResult guiText object 68
BLAgentBehaveLib.TreeType variable 169
bullet class 35, 36
Bullet object 201

C

CalculateNextMovementPoint() method 98
CalculateObstacles method 129
CalculatePath method 134, 135
C# FSM framework 29
chase state 43, 197
checkBet() method 71
cohesion rule 11
CompareTo method 125, 126
Component completion variable 180
conditional probability
  about 59
  loaded dice 60, 61

controller class 97
coroutine method 201
Cube game object 38

D

dead state 45, 46
DebugDrawGrid method 132
decorator 169, 170
Defense of the Ancient (DotA) 9
DetectAspect method 85
Dijkstra algorithm 28
direction property 114
Dynamic AI 64, 65

E

Enemy detected message 88
enemy tank AI
  about 39-41
  attack state 44
  chase state 43
  dead state 45
  patrol state 42
events component 8
Explosion property 36

F

FadeIn action 173
FadeOut action 174
FindNextPoint method 42
FindPath method 133
Finite State Machines. *See* FSM
FixedUpdate() method 68, 71
FlockController
  about 101-104
  code 101
flocking
  about 89
  from Unity Island Demo 89, 90
  implementing 99-101
followRadius 92
followVelocity 92
FSM
  about 7, 29, 159, 185, 194, 195
  abstract FSM class 38, 39
  attack state 198

chase state 197, 198
components 8
enemy tank AI 39
patrol state 195, 196
random 9
with probability 62-64
FSM, components
  events component 8
  rules component 8
  state component 8
  transitions component 8
FSMState class 49

G

Game Developers Conference (GDC) 12
GameObject.FindWithTag() method 188
GetColumn method 130
GetGridIndex method 129
GetNeighbours method 134
GetPoint method 111
GetRow method 130
GridManager class 123-129
GridManager object 128
guiText element 68
guiText object 58

H

HeuristicEstimateCost method 132
HFSM 159
hierarchical FSM. *See* HFSM
Hierarchical Task Networks. *See* HTNs
HTNs 159

I

Initialise method 83, 85
InstantiateTree method 166
InstantiateTree static method 166
intervalTime property 136
Is Looping flag 111

L

launcher weapon class 205
layers 116, 188
Length property 111

Locomotion 25-27

M

Manhattan length 15
map
  setting up 144
Max Slope property 150
messaging system 10
minimumDistToAvoid variable 120
missile launcher weapon 203, 204
mousePosition object 32

N

Natural language processing (NLP) 6
navigation mesh
  about 20-22, 144
  baking 145, 146
Navigation Static 145
navmesh. *See* navigation mesh
Nav Mesh Agent
  about 146, 147
  destination, updating 148
  Target.cs class 148, 149
  URL 147
NavMeshAgent array 149
NavMeshLayers
  about 151, 152
  creating 152
  new layer, adding 153
near miss 73, 74
Node class 125, 126
Node object 136
non-player characters (NPCs) 7
NPCTankController class 52, 53

O

obstacleList property 129
obstacles
  about 114
  avoiding 115-120
  custom layer, adding 116
Off Mesh Links
  about 153, 154
  generation 154, 155
  manual off 156

URL 157
OnDrawGizmos method 85, 111, 136
OnGUI() function 60
OnGUI method 117
OnGUI() method 58, 61, 64, 68
OnTriggerEnter event 86
OnTriggerEnter method 87

P

parallel node 179, 180
PARS 69
ParticleExplosion 36
path
  about 108, 110
  adding 108
  follower 111-114
  script 110, 111
pathArray property 136
Path.cs script 108
patrol state 42, 195
PatrolState class 50, 51
Paytable and Reel Strips. *See* PARS
PerformTransition method 52, 196
Perspective.cs file 83
perspective sense 83, 85
Physics.Raycast method 120
player car controller 190, 191
player tank 30
PlayerTankController class
  about 30
  bullet class 35, 36
  bullet, shooting 32
  properties 31, 32
  tank, controlling 32, 34
PlayerTankController.cs file
  code 31
PlayerTank.cs file 79
PlayerTank game object 30
PlayerTank script 79
playerTransform variable 192
polling 10
PriorityQueue class 123, 124, 126, 127
PriorityQueue.cs class 126
PRNG 56
probability
  about 56

conditional probability 59
defining 58
weighted probability 69-72
with FSM 62, 63
pseudorandom number generator. *See* **PRNG**
Pull Lever button 68

R

radius property 110
RAIN
URL 76
random
about 55, 56
class 56
dice game 57, 58
randomFreq 91
Random number generation. *See* **RNG**
randomPush value 91
Random.value property 56
range method 57
Raycast method 85, 119, 204
real-time strategy (RTS) game 9
recticle Player game object 187, 191
reference 181
Reset method 167
return to player. *See* **RTP**
Rigidbody component 30, 46
RNG 56
Robots project
versus Aliens project 181-184
RTP 69
rules component 8

S

scene
setting up 76, 77, 137-139, 186, 187
script
interfacing with 166, 168
seed property 56
selectors
about 175-177
priority selector 177-179
SelectTopPriority method 168, 177
sense class 83
Sense.cs file 83

sensors
implementing 75
sensor system 10, 76
separation rule 11
sequence 172
SetTransition method 51
Shoot method 200
ShouldDoMyAction decorator 170
s_Instance static variable 128
slope
scene, building with 149-151
slot machine
demo 65
random slot machine 65, 68, 69
Sort method 127
SpawnBullet method 201
SpawnMissile method 205
StartCoroutine method 93, 201
Start function 31
Start method 83, 112, 136
Start() method 70
state class 50
state component 8
statesPoll array 64
steering
about 12
layers 12, 13
steer() method 100, 101
Steer method 114
StopCoroutine method 201

T

tags 188
tank
controlling 32-34
Target.cs class 148
TargetMovement
about 104
file 104, 105
Target object 78, 80
targetTransform variable 80
target variable 102
Taxicab geometry. *See* **Manhattan length**
TestCode class 135, 136
throwLoadedDice() method 60
Tick method 167, 168

toOriginForce 92
toOriginRange 92
Touch.cs file 86
touch sense 86, 87
transitions component 8
Translate() method 96

U

Unity3D reference documentation
  URL 132
UnityFlockController entity 90
UnityFlock.cs file 91
UnityFlock script 90, 97
Unity Pro 143
Unity reference documentation
  URL 146
Unitys Island Demo
  flocking from 89, 90
Update method 82, 83, 113, 117, 118, 120,
      191, 206
Update() method 93, 100, 103
UpdateRandom() method 93
UpdateSense method 83, 85

V

Vector3.RotateTowards method 96
vehicles 189

W

WandarPoints 194
Wander.cs file 81
Wander script 82
waypoints
  setting up 37
WeaponGun class 191
WeaponMissile class 205
weapons
  about 199
  bullet object 201-203
  gun 200, 201
  launcher weapon 203-205
  missile 205, 206
weightedReelPoll array list 70
workflow 161-163

Thank you for buying
Unity 4.x Game AI Programming

About Packt Publishing

Packt, pronounced 'packed', published its first book "*Mastering phpMyAdmin for Effective MySQL Management*" in April 2004 and subsequently continued to specialize in publishing highly focused books on specific technologies and solutions.

Our books and publications share the experiences of your fellow IT professionals in adapting and customizing today's systems, applications, and frameworks. Our solution based books give you the knowledge and power to customize the software and technologies you're using to get the job done. Packt books are more specific and less general than the IT books you have seen in the past. Our unique business model allows us to bring you more focused information, giving you more of what you need to know, and less of what you don't.

Packt is a modern, yet unique publishing company, which focuses on producing quality, cutting-edge books for communities of developers, administrators, and newbies alike. For more information, please visit our website: www.packtpub.com.

Writing for Packt

We welcome all inquiries from people who are interested in authoring. Book proposals should be sent to author@packtpub.com. If your book idea is still at an early stage and you would like to discuss it first before writing a formal book proposal, contact us; one of our commissioning editors will get in touch with you.

We're not just looking for published authors; if you have strong technical skills but no writing experience, our experienced editors can help you develop a writing career, or simply get some additional reward for your expertise.

Unity 3.x Scripting

ISBN: 978-1-84969-230-4   Paperback: 292 pages

Write efficient, reusable scripts to build custom characters, game environments, and control enemy AI in your Unity game

1. Make your characters interact with buttons and program triggered action sequences

2. Create custom characters and code dynamic objects and players' interaction with them

3. Synchronize movement of character and environmental objects

4. Add and control animations to new and existing characters

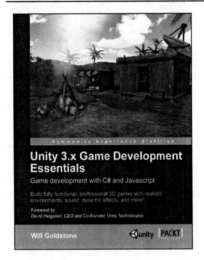

Unity 3.x Game Development Essentials

ISBN: 978-1-84969-144-4   Paperback: 488 pages

Build fully functional, professional 3D games with realistic environments, sound, dynamic effects, and more!

1. Kick start your game development, and build ready-to-play 3D games with ease.

2. Understand key concepts in game design including scripting, physics, instantiation, particle effects, and more.

3. Test & optimize your game to perfection with essential tips-and-tricks.

4. Learn game development in Unity version 3 and above, and learn scripting in either C# or JavaScript

Please check **www.PacktPub.com** for information on our titles

Unity 3 Game Development Hotshot

ISBN: 978-1-84969-112-3   Paperback: 380 pages

Eight projects specifically designed to exploit Unity's full potential

1. Cool, fun, advanced aspects of Unity Game Development, from creating a rocket launcher to building your own destructible game world

2. Master advanced Unity techniques such as surface shader programming and AI programming

3. Elite Unity programming for those looking to take their skills to the next level

Unity 3.x Game Development by Example Beginner's Guide

ISBN: 978-1-84969-184-0   Paperback: 408 pages

A seat-of-your-pants manual for building fun, groovy little games quickly with Unity 3.x

1. Build fun games using the free Unity game engine even if you've never coded before

2. Learn how to "skin" projects to make totally different games from the same file – more games, less effort!

3. Deploy your games to the Internet so that your friends and family can play them

4. Packed with ideas, inspiration, and advice for your own game design and development

Please check **www.PacktPub.com** for information on our titles

Lightning Source UK Ltd.
Milton Keynes UK
UKOW02f0903211113

221529UK00003B/87/P